Making the Best of Second Best

A Guide to Positive Stepparenting

Kathleen Fox

Published by
FoxCraft, Inc.
Box 7822
Rapid City, SD 57709

Published by

FoxCraft, Inc.
PO Box 7822
Rapid City, SD 57709

Copyright 1998 by Kathleen Fox
ISBN 0-9665543-0-2
Library of Congress Catalog Card Number 98-93251

Dedication

For Wayne, with gratitude for his love, support, and encouragement.

Acknowledgements

I am grateful to my husband for encouraging me to take risks and grow; to my children and stepchildren for enriching my life and teaching me more than they may ever realize; to Jamie for sharing her children with me so generously, and to members of the Poolside Group for their support.

Contents

Introduction

When I was a little girl I never once said to myself, "I want to be a stepmother when I grow up." It just isn't a job one aspires to, especially for those of us who learned about stepmothers from "Cinderella" and "Snow White."

But my life took some unexpected turns over the years, and eventually, without ever having planned it or prepared for it, I became a stepparent. This is a demanding job, and it has no formal training. I've never seen "Stepparenting 101" in a college catalog. I've never received a brochure in the mail advertising, "Learn to be a stepparent in the privacy of your own home for just pennies a day! Good jobs await our graduates!" (Thank goodness at least we do learn how to be stepparents in the privacy of our own homes. Some of those lessons include experiences we would never want known outside our own four walls.)

I've been doing on-the-job training in stepparenting for eight years now. I have two children (Loren is 21 and Rachel is 15 at this writing) and my husband has three (Stephanie is 18, Amy is 14, and Peter is 12). In the beginning of our stepfamilying, my kids lived with us all the time and his kids lived with us for half the year and with their mother for the other half. Over the years, we've had shifts in our living situations. When Loren was a sophomore in high school, he had an angry altercation with his stepdad and went to live with his father. A couple years later,

Stephanie decided life was easier at her mother's house and she preferred to live there full time. Right now Loren is in college and Stephanie is working and living on her own, with Rachel at our house all the time and Amy and Peter here for six months of the year.

I'm sure the details of your situation differ—maybe you're even like a friend of mine who has survived living in a blended family with six teenagers at once. Whatever your specific situation, we are sure to have feelings, issues, and concerns in common. Like trying to be fair, for instance. Or feeling caught in the middle. Or wondering if some of the kids in the family will ever decide to get along with each other.

These eight years haven't turned me into an "expert" with all the answers. But they have taught me a great deal. At least by now I'm beginning to figure out what the questions and the problems are.

One of the things I have learned along the way is that a blended family is inherently second best. Because of its many moving parts, the baggage brought into it by various family members, and the stresses and chaos which are part of it, a stepfamily is a tough place to do a good job of parenting. And the stepparent's place in the system is almost always second—in the eyes of society, in the view of the legal system, and in your stepkids' hearts. Most of the time, that's the right spot. Kids' biological parents certainly ought to come first.

But "second place" isn't the same as "no place." When you become a stepparent, you become part of your stepchildren's lives. You take on a responsibility to them as an authority figure and as a parent figure. They won't necessarily want you to assume that responsibility—on the contrary, they may battle you fiercely over it. But it's still your job. The specific dimensions of that job are often beyond your control, but you volunteered for it, and whether you succeed at it is largely up to you.

Despite the difficulties, it is certainly possible to build a functional, healthy stepfamily that is a good place for kids to grow up. It's the responsibility of both parents and stepparents to do their best to form that kind of family. The stepparent's role is often the hardest, and it may well be the most important. You are the one who has to build a relationship with your stepchildren, hang onto your relationship with your own children, and define your place in the new family. How well you do all of that is critical to the success of the blended family.

Creating a functional stepfamily isn't magic, and it isn't luck. It isn't one of those things that some people mysteriously can do while others can't. Making a blended family work takes work—as well as love, courage, humor, flexibility, and lots of energy. It also takes skills which can be learned and attitudes which can be changed.

Successful parents and stepparents concentrate on the positives. This doesn't mean going around with a phony smile, firmly insisting that everything is "just fine." It doesn't mean ignoring problems. It does mean overlooking the little things, dealing with the big things, and doing your best to figure out which is which. It means remembering that you are a volunteer in this situation. It means trying to hold onto the fact that you are an adult even when you don't feel capable of acting like one. It means building your skills, changing behaviors that don't work, and learning as you go. It means cultivating your sense of humor, your patience, and your ability to be flexible.

And above all, it means hanging in there. Stepfamilying is a long-term commitment. It is not to be taken on lightly or abandoned at the first sign of a struggle. A successful stepfamily isn't created in a month, or six months, or a couple of years. It grows slowly over time as the people in it learn to like, trust, and respect each other.

By now you may be ready to head out the door, convinced that working your heart out just to be second best isn't for you. Please stick around. The most important thing I've learned about stepfamilying is that it's a challenge well worth taking on. I'd like

3

to encourage you to think of stepparenting as an experience to appreciate and grow from, not merely endure.

Many of the books I have read about stepparenting emphasize the difficulties. Words such as "survival" and "coping" figure largely in their titles. But looking back over the past eight years has helped me realize how much I enjoy being part of a stepfamily as well as how much I have learned. Yes, the experience has often been difficult. Sometimes it has been exceedingly painful. It has also been a source of happiness, fulfillment, and a great deal of growth. I am a better person and a better parent now than I was then, and I'm grateful for the struggles that have helped me change (even though I didn't always appreciate them at the time).

I'd also like you to remember that what I am preaching here isn't necessarily what I'm always able to practice. As my kids and stepkids would be the first to tell you, I'm far from a perfect parent or stepparent. Much of this book includes lessons I have learned by doing things wrong the first time or strategies I wish I had known or practiced earlier. The book will have achieved one of its goals if it helps you avoid a few of the mistakes I have made along the way.

Stepfamilying is definitely a challenge. It contains more than its share of pain and heartache. Yet it can also provide many rewards and an abundance of joy. Choosing to work actively toward building a happy blended family can be one of the most rewarding things you will ever do in your life. Yes, maybe as a stepparent you will always be in second place. But I hope you'll come to appreciate, as I have, just how good a place second can be.

One

Second Best—
As Good as It's Going to Get

Congratulations! You have just been named a winner in the Stepparent Olympics. Some of the events in this spectacular competition include the Javelin (dodging pointed barbs tossed by resentful stepchildren), the Red Queen Marathon (running as hard as you can just to stay where you are), Gymnastics (twisting yourself into incredible contortions trying to stay out of the middle between your spouse and your children), and the Balance Beam Juggling event (trying to prove to your spouse, your kids, your stepkids, your ex-spouse, and your spouse's ex-spouse that you can do everything perfectly).

You've worked as hard as you could, you've put your heart and soul into the competition, and you've won your event. You step onto the platform, smiling through triumphant tears. And around your neck is placed—a silver medal.

In the Stepparent Olympics, you see, there is no such thing as going for the gold. Second place is as good as it's ever going to get.

For the sake of your own mental health, you might as well accept from the beginning that the stepfamily you are working so hard to build will always be second best. You as a stepparent will always be in second place. This doesn't mean you are doing a bad job, are a lousy parent, or are not good enough as a person. It just means that you are dealing with a difficult role in a situation that is far from perfect.

5

Ideally, all children would grow up in their original families with both their parents, who would be emotionally healthy, functional adults. Unfortunately, that isn't the case for many kids. Too many children who live with both parents are in abusive or dysfunctional families. And most children with divorced parents have been in such families. A stepfamily headed by mature, healthy adults who do effective parenting is certainly far better for kids than a biological family headed by abusive drug addicts or neglectful parents. So it definitely isn't true to say that it would be better for all kids to stay in their original biological families.

But even if a particular stepfamily is healthier than a particular original family, it is still not an ideal situation. One reason for this is simply its more complicated structure. You are dealing with two households instead of one, different rules and expectations, divorced parents who may still resent one another, angry kids, parents who don't present a united front, ample opportunities for manipulation, and conflicting loyalties. It is just plain hard to make all those moving parts function well together.

The second reason is the bond that exists between children and their biological parents. Mom and Dad aren't loved because they are good parents; they're loved because they are Mom and Dad. Even if Dad is an abusive alcoholic or Mom hasn't been around since the child was three, the bond and the love are still there. They may be tangled up with enough resentments and pain to keep a therapist busy for years, but they still exist.

You as a stepparent don't have that same birth bond with your stepchildren. You have to establish a new one—a formidable task, considering the many factors opposing it. Your stepkids are likely to view you as an intruder and resent you, especially in the beginning. If you have children of your own, they will be jealous of and resist your attempts to open your heart to make room for your stepkids. Your spouse may not want you invading his or her territory by getting too involved with the kids. Stepkids may feel that liking you is being disloyal to their other parent. The conflict generated by these feelings of divided loyalty may last for years, even if the stepchild comes to genuinely love you and appreciate the parenting you do.

So, given all those complicating elements, you might as well face the fact that you are second best. You may eventually be loved, you may be appreciated (some day, most likely when your stepkids have children of their own), you may be respected—but you aren't Mom or Dad. And, of course, you shouldn't be. Logically, it makes sense that a child's biological parents should come first. After all, you would hardly expect your own children to love a stepparent as much as they love you. All the logic in the world, though, doesn't make it any easier when you feel as if you're being pushed away despite all of your best efforts.

The reminders of your status can often be painful. An example of this is Connie's description of her feelings at her stepdaughter's wedding: "Allison has lived with her father and me ever since she was seven; she considers our house her home and just visits at her mother's. When she came down the aisle on her father's arm and handed only her mother a rose, I felt a tiny stab of disappointment."

A stab, indeed. Connie has done most of the mothering in Allison's life and loves her stepdaughter dearly. She is the one who has coped with the strep throats, the school projects, the dance lessons and soccer practices, and the struggles of adolescence. She has given her heart, her effort, and her time. She knows clearly that her love is reciprocated. Yet, in Allison's heart, her mother still comes first.

That is one of the realities of being a stepparent. No matter how good a stepparent you may be, how involved you are, or how much your stepchildren may actually come to love you, there is still a place in their hearts that you cannot and should not fill. However, if you're willing to be patient—and if you think it's worth the effort—you can make a place for yourself there.

Why Bother?

So is it worthwhile to work hard to make a place for yourself that will never be more than second best? The cliché is that when you're number two, you try harder. In a stepfamily, though, trying harder will never get you higher than number two. Nobody's ever going to give you a gold medal. And as if that isn't bad enough, you'll need to put forth all of your effort just to stay second.

The logical question then becomes, why on earth should you bother?

That's a good question. I ask it of myself regularly, when the chaos grows overwhelming or all the kids are mad at me at once or I don't get my way. On those days when I'm convinced this whole idea was a terrible mistake and we are never going to be a "real" family, the effort involved in being part of a stepfamily seems like just too much.

Even though I don't want to admit it on such days, the "why bother?" question does have an answer. Several answers, in fact. Here are a few of them; you may have others of your own.

1. Because even if a good original family is better than a good stepfamily, a good stepfamily is better than a bad original family or a bad stepfamily—and a bad stepfamily is simply awful. You wouldn't wish that kind of family on your kids, your stepkids, or yourself. If you get discouraged by the thought of being second best, does that mean you'd be willing to settle for sixth best or tenth best or 23rd best?

2. Because you get out of stepparenting what you put into it. If you are willing to do what you can to help create a successful stepfamily, it will be a far pleasanter place for you as well as for your kids and stepkids.

3. Because through working hard to be the best stepparent you can, you will learn some valuable things about being a better person. You will become more tolerant, more flexible, more understanding, and more accepting.

8

4. Because, preachy as it might sound, it's simply the right thing to do. You and your spouse chose to create this stepfamily. The children in it didn't. Therefore, it's your responsibility to make that family as good a place for those children as you can. The payoff is that, in the attempt, you also make the family a better place for yourself.

Work Within the Realities of Second Best

The factors that make a stepfamily second best also make it different from a traditional family. It's a setup for failure if you try to squeeze your stepfamily into the mold of a successful "typical" family that is made up of mother, father, and 2.5 darling children. It works much better to accept the reality that a stepfamily carries a load of old baggage, conflicting loyalties, resentments, complexity, and chaos that is not part of the makeup of a traditional family. It will never become just like an ordinary nuclear family. Even if you, your spouse, and all your joint kids and stepkids live in the same household all the time, your family won't bond in the same way or have the same dynamics as members of a biological family.

You can spend huge amounts of energy trying to make your stepfamily look just like a traditional family and trying to pretend that the built-in stepfamily issues will go away. Or you can accept the fact that a stepfamily is a stepfamily, with all the inherent difficulties. Then you can work around some of those difficulties, learn to live with others, and even change others from liabilities to assets. Let's take a look at a few examples of stepfamily realities and how you might deal with them.

1. Kids living in multiple households, with different rules and expectations. This adds a great deal of chaos and confusion, but it can have some positives, especially if the adults involved don't make it a bigger deal than it needs to be. Kids are more adaptable than you might think. After all, they have different rules at school, at grandparents' houses, and at friends' houses. The big advantage

here is that the kids learn to be flexible. As long as the rules are clear and reasonable at your house, don't worry about whether they match those at the other parents' houses.

2. Bitter former spouses who may try to sabotage your marriage and turn kids against you. There's not much you can do to turn this one into a positive. Be honest with the kids and keep the lines of communication open as much as you can. Treat the ex-spouse politely even if your courtesy isn't returned. Recognize that time is your friend here. Over time, the bitterness is likely to fade. And as kids get older, they are capable of sorting out for themselves what is the truth and what is maliciousness born from old resentment.

3. Angry stepkids. Recognize as best you can that the anger doesn't usually have anything to do with you as a person. Put yourself in the child's place and imagine how you would feel. Accept that an angry outburst is sometimes the first step toward solving a problem. Anger can be channeled into something constructive; passive resentment and withdrawal are often easier to handle in the short term but more destructive in the long term.

4. Kids' bonds with their biological parents. You can't fight it, so you might as well encourage it. Allow kids to feel free to call their other parent from your house, to talk about that parent, to bring gifts from that parent to your house, and the like. Don't try to push yourself into the parent's spot; instead, think of yourself as a teacher or mentor or friend. Remember that your goal here is not to be better than the other parent; it is to have you and your stepkids all be comfortable living together. If they need some contact with their other parent in order to be comfortable, it's probably in your best interest as well as theirs to let them have it.

5. Conflicting loyalties. Never make your kids choose between you and their other parent. Never expect kids to spy on your ex-spouse for you or pump them for information on what goes on at the other parents' house. Never try to make your stepkids love you more than they love their parents. Take the high road

every time on this one. You'll be easing conflict and setting a good example for the kids.

6. Multiple sets of parents and extended families. This can create conflict, of course, because of parents' and stepparents' different points of view and beliefs. But it can also be turned into a strength. Each parent, stepparent, or grandparent has something unique to offer the kids in terms of discipline, values, skills, or interests. The kids have extra adult role models who care about them. Think of it this way—if it takes a village to raise a child, a stepfamily has its own built-in village.

If a stepfamily shouldn't and can't become just like a typical nuclear family, then what can you use as a model for your blended family? How do you know whether your stepfamily is successful? Because there are so many variations in stepfamilies, it's hard to come up with one definition of a successful one. Each family almost needs to create its own. However, I believe most successful stepfamilies would have the following characteristics:

1. The new couple are both emotionally finished with their former marriages, whether those marriages ended because of death or divorce. They are not still actively grieving, filled with unresolved resentment toward a former spouse, or wishing the first marriage hadn't ended.

2. The couple is the strongest unit in the blended family—husband and wife come first for each other, support each other, and work together to parent the kids.

3. Family members communicate. The communication may not always be sweetly reasonable, but it moves toward getting a problem solved instead of getting stuck in cycles of blaming or complaining. Problems and conflicts are addressed and dealt with as effectively as possible, instead of being ignored, covered up, or grimly endured.

4. There is cooperation or at least polite communication with former spouses. Even if the relationship isn't friendly, it is primarily based on what is best for the children. If someone's

former spouse is still hostile or bitter, that hostility isn't allowed to carry over into the present family.

5. The adults in the family are willing to get help for themselves and the children when it is needed—whether that's a stepfamily support group, a 12-step group, a church family, or individual or family counseling.

6. The adults set an example of courtesy, flexibility, openness, and tolerance over small matters. The family doesn't waste a lot of time and energy in power struggles over minor issues.

7. All the kids are given clear boundaries and limits. No matter how parents and stepparents divide parenting duties or authority, it is clear that the adults are in charge. Kids aren't allowed to run wild or dominate the family because parents or stepparents feel guilty over past mistakes, try to compete with a former spouse for the kids' love, try too hard to be liked, or don't have the courage to make the tough choices that parenting demands.

8. Things improve with time. Conflicts ease as family members get used to being part of a household and accept one another. Stepsiblings learn to like or at least tolerate each other, while stepkids and stepparents develop bonds. The family isn't rehashing the same problems after six years that it was struggling with at six months.

9. Not every conflict, struggle, or difficulty is seen as a stepfamily issue. Some of them are recognized as part of the natural order of things in any family as people live together and kids grow up.

10. Family member enjoy good times together—everything isn't conflict and tension all the time or even most of the time.

If most of the characteristics above apply to your family most of the time, then you're probably doing well. In the areas where you would like to improve, remember to set goals based on how your family functions rather than how it looks. Because there are so many possible living arrangements, you just can't fit a successful stepfamily into a predefined box. So don't try. Fit the characteristics above to your particular family instead of trying to fit your family into someone else's list.

The Time to Start is Now

Becoming a better parent or stepparent is a bit like beginning an exercise program or losing 25 pounds—tomorrow always seems to be the best time to get started. We'll be more patient someday, when we're not so stressed out at work. We'll take all the kids camping so we can get to know them better when we have more time. We know we should listen more and yell less, and we'll work on that—one of these days.

I think of this as the "Scarlett O'Hara Syndrome." Remember in *Gone With the Wind* how she was always going to be a lady someday? When the war was over, she would be kind and gentle and patient like her mother. But when the time came, she couldn't do it. She didn't know how, because she had been practicing just the opposite all those years.

It would be great if we were rewarded for our good intentions by suddenly waking up one morning transformed into perfect stepparents. Unfortunately, it doesn't work that way. We have to put our intentions into action, one step at a time.

There are two keys to making changes effectively. One is to be specific about what you want to do differently. The other is to start small, but start now.

If your goal is a vague intention to "get along better with my stepkids," you aren't likely to get far. Instead, set a specific goal. Phrase it in positive terms—what you will do instead of what you won't do. Changing a behavior is easier if you replace it with a better one rather than trying to give it up cold turkey.

Establish your goal clearly in your own mind. It may help to write it down. You might have something like, "I will speak to the kids in a pleasant voice instead of yelling so much."

Then, even more important, figure out your first specific action toward this goal. For example: "Tonight I will tell Jenny goodnight without scolding her about her messy room." "If the kids are fighting, I will give them each a time-out instead of yelling at them."

Make sure your first step is small enough to do easily. Then do it—even if today is a busy day, or you're tired, or the kids are going out of the way to be difficult. When you've made that change successfully for a few days, add another step. Then another. And eventually you'll be the kind of stepparent you want to be.

We have a tape of children's music called *God's Project* which includes a song titled, "Change Your Thoughts and You Can Change Your World." When Stephanie, then age nine, first heard the song, she thought the words were "Change Your Socks and You Can Change Your World." The kids have sung it that way ever since. I think the amended version makes sense, because if you are going to change your life, just thinking different thoughts isn't enough. Yes, you have to start there—by shifting your attitude, deciding on a goal, and wanting to change. But you don't get anywhere until you take some action to change the smelly old socks of your bad habits.

Therapist and author Earnie Larsen is fond of saying, "If nothing changes, nothing changes." Thinking about change, talking about change, or intending to change don't accomplish a thing if that's all we do. Change is *doing something different.* And it doesn't happen tomorrow, it happens today.

Two

The Foundation

In third grade my daughter Rachel and stepdaughter Amy made family trees. Amy's tree included her mother, her father, her sister and her brother—period. Rachel's tree included her father, me, her stepdad, her brother, her stepsisters and stepbrother, Amy's stepbrothers and stepsister on her mother's side, our cat, and Amy's stepdad's dog. Defining a family isn't quite as simple as it used to be.

Most of us still think of a "family" as Mom and Dad and their children. This traditional kind of a family usually grows over time in a more or less orderly fashion. A man and woman get married. Later they begin having children—almost always one at a time. The children show up as babies, ready to bond with their parents and with their places in the family already defined. This kind of family is like building a new house. There are blueprints to follow, the construction starts with a foundation, and the rest of the structure is added one component at a time.

But creating a blended family doesn't follow this tidy pattern. It's more like remodeling—trying to make the new modern kitchen compatible with the antique French doors or fit the Jacuzzi tub into the bathroom that used to be a pantry. Nobody has any blueprints that match anything. And goodness knows what you're likely to find when you start digging into the old wiring or plumbing.

A stepfamily's beginning is abrupt. Even if a couple have known each other for some time, the reality of joining together as a family means a challenging adjustment. A stepfamily may include children who have still been hoping Mom and Dad will get back

15

.sed to be the oldest but who have suddenly ved to second or third oldest, children who up the closeness they have developed living as a single parent, stepsiblings who don't like arents who have different ideas on child-rearing, s. don't know how to be parents because they have no chn their own—and on and on. And we have the nerve to call this conglomeration a "blended family."

It blends, all right. So do grapefruit and black olives if you put them into the blender and turn the power on for a while. But that doesn't necessarily mean the results are going to be pretty. So before you dump everybody together and hit the "on" switch, it's helpful to have a little understanding of the foundation of a stepfamily.

A Foundation of Pain as Well as Joy

It's tempting to pretend that in creating a stepfamily we are starting from scratch with a brand-new family. But the truth is that we aren't. It's important to accept the fact that a blended family has its foundations in pain and loss as well as joy and hope. Each member of a stepfamily brings along his or her own expectations, resentments, and fears. The new couple, despite some fears and concerns, will most likely be in love, happy with each other, and optimistic. Their children may well be angry, resentful, jealous, and afraid.

Most stepfamilies today are created by partners who have been divorced. Those divorces didn't just happen for no reason. Most commonly, they were the result of abuse, addiction, emotional immaturity, or some other dysfunction. A family which has problems in any of these ways is a difficult place for a child to grow up. A divorce, even if it may be a step toward improving the unhealthy situation, causes further pain for both kids and adults. So by the time everyone gets to the point of a new marriage and a blended family, they have all been more or less battered by circumstances. This pain is an integral part of the foundation of any stepfamily. You need to acknowledge it if you want the stepfamily to function well.

All I need to do to remind myself of the pain on which a stepfamily rests is look through old family photo albums. There are all the memories. Loren as a week-old baby with his father and me beaming fondly. All of us with Gary's family. All of us with my family. Rachel as a baby with her proud big brother. Birthday parties. Family Christmas celebrations.

But after a few years the pictures change. Loren and Rachel with Dad. Loren and Rachel with me. None of all of us together. There is the record of a family coming apart. The pain shows in the eyes behind the smiles in some of those pictures. In them, I see two kids who used to live in a family affected by the tension and pain of alcoholism. But I also see kids who loved both their parents and wanted to be with both of us.

I can remember how painful it was for me to go through a divorce. But even though I was there when they went through it, I can't know the depth of the pain my children felt when their father and I separated. I can only imagine it, just as I can only imagine the pain my stepchildren have known. And doing my best to imagine that pain is an important thing for me to do every now and then. It helps me feel more compassion for the struggles they all have had in learning to live as part of a stepfamily.

A child's resentment and rudeness toward a stepmother may grow out of the pain of realizing, because of this marriage, that Dad really isn't ever going to get back together with Mom. Jealousy of a new stepsister is a natural reaction to having to share Mom's love and time. Children who are rebellious and angry, refusing to accept a new blended family, aren't just being bad or difficult. They hurt, and they need some help.

That doesn't mean it's okay to vandalize a new stepfather's car or abuse a stepsister or call a stepmother ugly names. It's not an acceptable excuse for parents and stepparents to abandon

17

discipline. But it does mean that children need compassion as well as consequences.

Compassion and Empathy

Genuine compassion is a mature emotion. Children, even when they are kind and caring, don't have the depth of experience to have developed it. It's helpful if you as a stepparent can show enough compassion for both of you. This is particularly important in your first months and years as a stepfamily. And, of course, that's precisely the time when being compassionate and understanding is the hardest.

I remember some of my feelings and internal struggles as a new stepparent. I would have liked some time alone to build and enjoy my new relationship with Dean. I felt rejected and pushed away by Loren, who was still angry at me for divorcing his dad and who kept accusing me of favoring my stepkids over my own kids. I felt challenged by Stephanie, who resented my authority and seemed to want me out of her dad's life. I was trying to give the three younger kids the time and energy they needed as they adjusted to the upheavals in their lives. I was afraid that if our new stepfamily wasn't perfect, Dean and I would both lose custody of our kids and it would be my fault. And I was trying to live up to my self-assigned role of Supermom and SuperStepmom.

Looking back now, with a combination of relief, amusement, and understanding, I can see how overwhelming all of that was. If someone had come along and told me, "You need to be more compassionate toward your kids and stepkids," I'd have hit them over the head with whatever stepfamily book I was reading at the time.

But now, safely removed by several years, that's exactly what I'm preaching. It's easier for me to be compassionate and understanding now toward both the scared kids who lived in our house eight years ago and the insecure adults who were trying to do a good job as parents and stepparents. It wouldn't have been nearly as easy back then. It might have helped if I had used some of the following strategies:

1. Put yourself in the child's place. How would you feel if you were ten and your parents divorced? How would you react if you had to share your room with a stranger? How would you feel if you and Mom had been united against the world and then suddenly Mom invited someone else in and pushed you out? Ask yourself these questions over and over again. Practice seeing the other person's perspective until it becomes a habit. It will help you handle conflicts with more empathy and understanding.

2. Find a safe place to express your own hurts, frustrations, and fears. The best place for this is a stepfamily support group such as those affiliated with the Stepfamily Association of America. If one isn't available in your community, perhaps you could help start one. This is the best choice for support because you can benefit from the experiences of others who are also members of stepfamilies. But there are also many other options. Try a 12-step group, a church group, a counselor, a therapy group, or a network of close friends. When you can get support outside the family for your own struggles, it's easier for you to maintain the energy and strength you need within the family.

3. Remind yourself, "They're only children." Even if your stepkids are teenagers, they aren't as big and powerful as they may seem to you. They may be great manipulators or skilled strategists, but they still have limited experience and shallow perspectives. They are just children, doing their best to cope in a difficult situation. It's simply an unfortunate fact of stepfamily life that their coping may involve trying to get rid of you by making your life miserable.

4. Pay attention to what kids are trying to gain, not just what they are doing. A useful technique is to ask, "What will getting that do for them?" Suppose your stepson and stepdaughter, both the oldest in their birth families, are fighting for the dominant position in the new stepfamily. What will gaining that position do

for them? Perhaps it would gain them respect, power, or a sense of being in control. Once you arrive at an answer, then you might be able to think of more constructive ways they could both get what they want.

5. Remember that compassion goes from the strong to the weak. Empathy and victimhood don't coexist well at all. Everything you do to build compassion for your stepchildren will also work to reduce your own sense of helplessness and strengthen your own internal position.

6. As a corollary to number five, don't mistake compassion for spinelessness and allow yourself to be abused or run over. Feeling compassion for your stepkids isn't the same thing as letting them take over the household or turn into bullies.

Developing more compassion for the children in your blended family isn't necessarily intended to change your actions. What it can change is your attitude. If you see these kids as struggling little people in the middle of a painful and difficult situation, you will react differently than you will if you see them as powerful little monsters who are out to get you. You will still get angry with them, have your feelings hurt, get into power struggles, and hack your way through conflicts. But through all of those hassles, you will be able to take the struggles less personally, because of your awareness of the pain that lies beneath their behavior.

The Strongest Link

A blended family is actually a system made up of a number of smaller units. Family therapist Jamie Keshet calls these "minifamilies," which she defines as a family unit smaller than a nuclear family because its slots (father, mother, child) are not all filled. She considers the former spouses a minifamily because of the need for joint parenting. She discusses minifamilies in more detail in her excellent book, *Love and Power in the Stepfamily* (McGraw-Hill, 1987).

In our family, for example, we have the following minifamilies: my husband Dean and me, Dean and his three kids, and my two kids and me. Then the kids all belong to other units with their other parents. Each one has its own set of traditions, expectations, and boundaries.

After a divorce, each parent forms a new minifamily with the kids. The balance of power often shifts, with the kids having more of a voice than they did when both parents were present. There can be a sense of closing ranks against outsiders.

When a parent remarries, this family unit has to change again. Those closed ranks need to open to let in the stepparent. Changing the boundaries of several minifamilies to create a new family unit is part of the stress stepfamilies have to cope with. In the beginning, the various minifamilies are often stronger than the blended family as a whole, and they can get tangled up in destructive power struggles.

There are two keys to preventing such power struggles from destroying the new blended family before it grows strong enough to have its own identity. One is communication, strongly seasoned with respect for the traditions and history of the other minifamilies. Combining everyone's holiday traditions to create new ones is an example of this. The other key is for the new couple to become the strongest unit. In order for our blended family to become a functional system, my loyalty to my husband and his to me must come before our allegiance to the minifamilies we each have with our own children.

Sometimes it's appropriate for various minifamilies to break off for a time. The death of a relative, for example, may involve a mother and her children but only marginally affect her husband and his children. This kind of splitting off doesn't threaten the overall stepfamily unit because it's temporary. But more long-term divisions can create serious problems.

When I met Marian at a workshop, her blended family was struggling over this very issue. The main problem, she told me, was conflict between her husband and her youngest child, a teenage son. "My kids and I married this man a few years ago," she said, "and now he doesn't even speak to Todd except to criticize him. I tell Todd he's a senior and only has to hang in there for a few more months, but it's getting really tough."

In our brief conversation, I didn't find out a lot of details about Marian and her family. But her tone of voice and choice of words gave me some clues about the possible source of some of their problems.

The first red flag was her phrase, "My kids and I married this man." Marriage is a contract and commitment between two people, not between two family units. You marry your spouse; your kids don't. They come along for the ride, quite possibly against their wishes.

But Marian evidently entered into her second marriage with a perception that her new husband was one party to the arrangement and she and her kids together made up the second party. She still thought of herself and her kids as a unit separate from her husband. It would be natural for her kids to be reluctant to open ranks and let a stepfather into the single-parent minifamily. The real problem arose because Marian was reluctant to let him in, as well. Her primary loyalty was still to the minifamily unit of herself and her kids.

Several years after their marriage, the weakness of Marian's commitment to her husband was evident. During our conversation, she never referred to her spouse as "my husband" or by his name. It was always, "this man I married"—in approximately the tone someone would use to say, "this root canal I had."

I don't know enough about Marian's family to make a judgment about the causes of their problems. But I wonder what different tone of voice she might have had for "this man she married" had she been clearer in the beginning about just who was marrying whom. The most powerful unit in that stepfamily was not the one made up of Marian and her husband; it was the one made up of Marian and her children. Maybe, after several years of conflict, it was too late for this blended family to survive. Or maybe the departure of Marian's youngest son for college would give the husband-wife unit a chance to thrive and perhaps even eventually make room for the adult children in a different way.

Family units will continue to shift in various ways as the blended family evolves. Perhaps an ex-spouse who has been only marginally involved with the kids moves back to town and wants to be closer to them. Maybe a teenager who has always spent summers with her father in another state won't want to do that any more as she gets older and becomes more involved with summer jobs and friends. Maybe younger and older kids in a blended family will develop their own factions based on age rather than biological relationship. And the first time all of your kids and stepkids join forces in opposition to you and your spouse, celebrate. It's a sign that they're bonding into a family.

Ideally, in the process of all this shifting, the various minifamilies will combine more or less closely into one overall unit, the stepfamily. Keeping that merger as the overall goal, but recognizing the existence of the other families, is a helpful way for parents and stepparents to hang onto the flexibility that is so important to the survival of a stepfamily.

It can also be extremely useful to talk with kids, especially younger ones, about the idea of each of us belonging to several different families. It helps them accept differences in family traditions, rules, and behaviors. It reduces the pressure they feel to choose one family or one parent over another. When the blended family incorporates a child's various minifamilies rather than replacing them, it's easier for the child to accept becoming part of the new overall family unit.

Three

How Do I Fit In Here?

Job Descriptions, Please

When Amy was in first grade, she explained carefully, so as not to hurt my feelings, that she was giving the Mother's Day gift she made in school to her mom, "because she's my real Mom and you're my other Mom."

Just what being the "other Mom" or "other Dad" means is something each blended family must establish for itself. That job description varies greatly depending on custody arrangements, children's ages, and the involvement of the kids' other parents. If you are the stepfather of a five-year-old girl who lives with you and rarely sees her dad, you may virtually be her father. If you are the stepmother of a 16-year-old boy who only visits occasionally, you are unlikely to develop a mother/son relationship with him. Neither of you may even want or need a friendship; mutual tolerance may be about as far as you go.

Even if you don't develop a close relationship with your stepchildren because of ages or distance, you still are part of their lives and they are part of yours. When you marry someone, your intention is to make a lifetime commitment to each other. If your spouse has children, they are included in your lifetime commitment. For better or worse, even if you don't intend to have a whole lot to do with one another, you have become part of the same family. Your challenge is to figure out just what place in the family belongs to you.

Your role as a stepparent will develop and evolve over time. But rather than just passively letting it happen, it's a good idea for you to work with your spouse and actively create it. You don't have to fit yourself into the corners and accept whatever role other family members let you have or think you should have. It's your responsibility to figure out and take on a place in the family that fits best for you as well as for your spouse and stepkids.

As you're developing that role, pay more attention to what you want to *do* than how you think you should *be*. Don't get locked into "what a stepmother or stepfather is." Instead, use the perspective of "what do I need to do to help everyone in this family become comfortable together." Maybe a book about stepfamilies says, "stepparents should leave discipline to the biological parent." Maybe a friend who grew up in a stepfamily says, "stepfathers should back off and not try too hard to be involved with their stepkids." If a piece of advice like this fits your situation, that's fine. If it doesn't, then forget about it. Just work toward being a positive and consistent presence in your stepkids' lives in whatever way works for your family.

"Jeff, This is My Er, Um.."

While you're busy defining your job description in the stepfamily, you might want to give a thought to what your title should be. Make it a passing thought, though. In some families, this question seems to get more attention than I believe it deserves. Books often suggest that the stepparent should be called Mom or Dad plus their name, which might work well for some families. It seems clumsy as well as unnecessary to me. "Mommy Kathleen" is too young for our kids, "Mom Kathleen" is simply awkward, and "Mother Kathleen" sounds too much like I just left the convent. One woman, only a few years older than her teenage stepchildren, decided along with the kids that she would be called their "stepfriend." For them that designation worked well because it

25

was simple and it fit the role she wanted to have in their lives. Some families experiment with nicknames, which can work as long as everyone is comfortable with them and they aren't obnoxiously cute.

In most cases, though, I don't see a need for stepfamilies to expend much energy on making up titles or hassling about what to call one another. When I first met Dean's kids, he introduced me simply as "Kathleen." (That wasn't planning; it just didn't occur to us to do anything else.) And that's been good enough ever since. I'm sure in the beginning I had my fair share of being called *Her* in a dreadfully significant tone behind my back. There was an occasional pointed statement like, "Is *She* coming along, too?" just to remind me of my status as an interloper. That's part of the package for almost any stepparent.

But by now Dean's kids all introduce me comfortably as "my stepmom." If I leave a note for all the kids, I sign it "Mom/Kathleen." If I'm in a store with Peter and a clerk says something about "your mom," the mistake isn't important enough for either of us to correct. We both know who his mom really is, so we don't worry about it. If teachers or new friends assume I am Amy's mom or Dean is Rachel's dad, the kids matter-of-factly explain the correct relationship.

If you are the stepparent of small children whose biological parent has died or is completely absent, it may be appropriate to work toward having them call you Dad or Mom. But in most stepfamilies, where kids already have a mother and father in the picture, it's silly to add unnecessary stress by expecting stepkids to call you "Mom" or "Dad." All you'll do is build resentment from both the kids and the other parent. Don't cause extra hassles for your stepfamily by creating a conflict over this issue. It isn't necessary to invent a cutesy name or fight with anybody about what to call you. Keep it simple—just use your name, call yourself a stepmother or stepfather, and save your energy for the real problems.

While you're dealing with all those real problems, though, don't forget that there are some advantages to being the "other parent." The woman who decided to be a "stepfriend" was able to build close and comfortable relationships with her teenage stepchildren by not trying to be their parent. Stepparents sometimes get to sidestep the mother-daughter or father-son conflicts of adolescence. Because you are more detached from your stepkids, you don't feel so personally responsible for their hurts or mistakes or misbehavior. This means you can sometimes be more effective than their parents in providing support or enforcing consequences.

There are times when I like being in second place instead of front and center. It was easier for Stephanie to practice driving with me than with her dad, for example. I can react with more detachment—and therefore sometimes more practical help—if one of Dean's kids is in trouble. And when Peter was supposed to choose a volunteer to do the "chicken dance" with him at his kindergarten program, he picked his mother instead of me.

You're Not the Boss of Me!

"You're not my parent!"

There can't be a stepparent anywhere in the world who hasn't been reminded of that fact at least once. The reminder is usually followed by some variation of, "And you can't tell me what to do!"

So what do you do when your authority is challenged this way? First of all, agree. "You're right, I'm not your parent." (Please try to resist the temptation to add, "Thank God!")

But don't let yourself be conned into believing that "parent" and "authority figure" are synonyms. After all, these kids' lives are full of non-parent adults, from teachers to babysitters to bus drivers, who can and do regularly tell them what to do. You don't have to be a child's parent to be able to enforce rules or set boundaries. If you are an adult in a household where stepchildren live or visit, you have every right to receive respect, courtesy, and obedience from those children.

It's a mistake for stepparents, especially new ones or those who aren't involved with their stepkids on a daily basis, to try to assume more authority than they have. But it's just as big a mistake not to use the authority they do have.

Knowing exactly what that authority is, of course, is where the problem comes in. For biological parents, the expectations are usually reasonably clear for both children and adults. Even when kids rebel against parental authority, at least they know the authority is there or is supposed to be there. For stepparents, it's a lot tougher. At the same time you are trying to enforce rules and teach discipline, you are trying to make friends and "sell yourself" as being a good person.

This is a delicate and difficult balancing act. And while you're up there on the tightrope with your pitifully inadequate umbrella, doing your best to get across without falling into the "too-friendly" void on one side and the "too-rigid" pit on the other, your stepkids are busy shaking the rope at one end while your kids are pulling on it at the other. If you're lucky, your spouse is holding out a safety net, or at least shouting encouragement.

What makes this tightrope act even harder is that no one outside your family can really tell you how to do it. Any advice you get has to be adapted to your particular situation. But, of course, that's not going to stop me from offering you some advice. See which of these suggestions fit for your stepfamily:

1. Almost every book and article on stepfamilying I've ever read suggests that discipline in the beginning should be reserved for the biological parent. Do I think that's good advice? Yes. Is that the way we did it? No. Since Dean's job is a demanding one which includes some traveling, and since I was home with the kids, I did a great deal of the parenting with his kids from the first. I can't honestly say, looking back now, whether that was the best choice. I do know that it's what we did, it worked reasonably well, and it fit our circumstances at the time.

2. Don't try so hard to be a friend that you forget to be an authority figure. Yes, you want your stepkids to like you. But you also need them to respect you. Be friendly, be pleasant, be fair—but be adult.

3. If you see your position with your stepkids as more of a "stepfriend" than a parent, be sure you don't undermine the authority of your spouse by pairing with the kids. If your choice is not to be actively involved as a parent, then stay out of the way and let your spouse do it. If you think you ought to intervene or question a decision because it isn't fair to the kids, do it privately with your spouse, never in front of the kids.

4. If you don't have children of your own, learn something about kids. Take a parenting class, talk to friends who are parents, or find some books on child development. It's easy as a stepparent to assume every hassle with kids is a stepfamily issue, when some of them are just a normal part of growing up.

6. Kids need parenting from somebody. Don't just let the kids run wild while you worry about who should do what or agonize over your job description. If nobody else is providing strong parenting, maybe you need to. Or maybe you need to stay out of the way but encourage your spouse to learn to be a stronger parent.

Whether you are actively or minimally involved in parenting, it's helpful to recognize that the parent/child relationship is inherently adversarial part of the time. The parents are supposed to teach discipline, provide protection, and set limits, which means that they are automatically going to come into conflict with their kids from time to time. No matter who is doing the parenting, somebody has to be the bad guy some of the time. Obviously, in the beginning it's better if that person can be the biological parent. As the stepfamily grows, the disciplinarian role can be shared.

One situation which can cause problems is when a single parent has abdicated parental authority and given up too much power to the kids. A stepparent (most often the stepfather) might be expected to come into this situation and "straighten those kids out." If you're being asked to take on this role, you're being handed a tough assignment. Before you accept it, have some serious discussion with your spouse. Even if it takes some sessions with a counselor or some parenting classes, it would be far better for the parent to learn how to be a stronger disciplinarian and take the lead in that area.

Regardless of whether your stepparenting role includes a lot of parenting or very little, your position needs to be made clear to the kids. It's the responsibility of the natural parent to let the kids know clearly that the stepparent is an authority figure who is to be respected and obeyed. Sometimes this can and should be done directly in words. "Whenever I'm not here, Paul is in charge."

But the parent's actions are far more important than words. If Stacy's stepmother says she has to finish her homework before she goes to the mall, and her father intervenes to say she can go, Stacy is being taught to disregard her stepmother. If Stacy's father thinks her stepmother is being unreasonable, they need to have a private discussion. Then if the decision is changed, Stacy needs to be told by her stepmother, not her father. It's crucial for the parent and stepparent to operate as a team.

The single parent and the kids have been a defined family unit. In order to make room for a new stepparent, that unit must change. Most kids don't want to let a stepparent in and will fight the change with intensity ranging from slight resistance to downright hostility. If your spouse doesn't want to let you in, either, then you have a real problem. In some stepfamilies, there is a clear rule, spoken or unspoken, that says, "I will discipline my own kids, and you keep out of it." That may be a perfectly appropriate arrangement for your stepfamily. However, since you are an adult living in the household, you still have a role there. It's essential to the health of the blended family for the natural parent to actively encourage and help define that role. Even if it doesn't include a lot of parenting, it needs to include some clear authority.

When one couple talked about how much authority the stepmother should have, they developed a useful strategy. The husband's teenage children visited in the summer rather than living in the household. Their stepmother found it worked well to treat them in much the same way she would treat visiting friends of her children. She enforced "house rules" which everybody was expected to follow—hang up your own bath towels, help with dishes, no loud radios, etc. She let her husband handle problems and conflicts over curfews, use of the car, fighting with siblings, etc. This kept the primary parenting responsibilities with the children's father, but supported the stepmother as someone to be respected and obeyed.

Finding a place in the family can be a particular challenge for new stepparents who are not already parents. Not only are they trying to become part of a new system, but they have to start learning how to be a parent in the middle instead of the beginning. Natural parents at least get in some trial-and-error practice while the kids are still too little to know what's going on. Pity the poor stepparent with no prior experience who walks into a household where children are older and have already graduated from Manipulation 202, Advanced Whining, and Outwitting Your Parent 305.

But though becoming an instant parent may be tough, it's not impossible. It can be done, and done well.

I know two stepfathers who had not been previously married and had no children. One has three teenage stepsons, the other a young stepson and stepdaughter. They both actively participate in parenting, and they're doing a great job. They have several things in common:

1. They both chose, with the support of their wives, to take on a parenting role. It's important to recognize that this is a choice. In these two families, one father lives a distance away and the other is only superficially involved with his children. So active involvement by the stepfathers is important. In some blended families, it may be more appropriate for stepparents to stay in the background when it comes to parenting. This is likely to be the

case when kids are older teenagers, or when their other natural parent has primary custody or is very much involved with them.

2. They communicate. This is essential! One of them participates in a support group. Both of them talk with the kids, listen to them, discuss issues with their wives, and aren't afraid to talk about struggles they have or apologize when they make mistakes.

3. Their spouses actively support them and encourage them to be involved with the kids. The natural parents aren't sending messages of, "These are my kids, so stay out of the way." The stepparents are considered part of the team.

Being part of the parenting team doesn't necessarily mean sharing the responsibility equally. It just means involving the stepparent in whatever way fits for that particular family. And it means defining the stepparent's authority as clearly as possible to help everyone in the family become more comfortable together.

Write Your Job Descriptions in Pencil

So you've survived the first months or couple of years in a stepfamily and you've figured out your role. What happens now? Why, it changes, of course. Just when you get your "other parent" job description figured out, it's almost certain to become obsolete. As kids get older, as living arrangements shift, as all the members of the blended family work out relationships with each other, the roles will change. In addition, your role might not necessarily be the same with different stepchildren.

In our blended family, I have always done a lot of the parenting with my husband's kids when they live with us. Because Dean's job includes some travel and because I work part-time at home, I am the one who's available to drive for the school field trip or help with spelling or make sure everyone does their chores. For us that arrangement works well. But even within our family, my parenting role has varied. When I first met them, Dean's kids were aged ten, five, and three. Stephanie accepted my role as an authority figure in her life reasonably well, although we had and still have some periods of serious conflict. But I don't think either of us has ever thought of our respective roles as mother/daughter ones. Because Amy and Peter were younger, I have been much more involved as a parent figure, have become much closer to them, and have probably had more influence in their lives than has been the case with Stephanie.

Parenting job descriptions aren't the only ones that need to be defined in a stepfamily. Kids' roles change, as well. In our family, for example, Stephanie was the oldest child among Dean's kids. A strong personality, she babysat for the younger ones, bossed them unmercifully, and was very much aware of her in-charge position. In our blended family, all of a sudden she was the second oldest kid, and she didn't like it one bit. Many of our hassles in the early days involved power struggles between Stephanie and Loren. The conflict eased with time, but didn't really end until Loren moved to his father's house. That left Stephanie in full possession of the field, and she once again took over her role as the oldest kid. Had Loren stayed in our household, the two of them would probably have continued to spar for position and perhaps would eventually have come to some sort of reconciliation.

Rachel was the youngest in our family. All of a sudden, when Amy and Peter became part of our lives, she turned into a middle child and a big sister. This transition wasn't as difficult as the struggle between the two oldest kids, but it still meant some changes. Even Amy, who stayed in the middle, and Peter, who remained the youngest, found that the job descriptions for those positions had changed.

If you are particularly interested in the issue of birth-order conflicts in your stepfamily, there is some useful discussion of the subject in Dr. Kevin Leman's book *Living in a Stepfamily Without Getting Stepped On.* He discusses the role of birth order in the way people react to one another, applying it both to spouses and to the children in a stepfamily.

Of course, children's roles change in many ways in addition to their birth order. An only child may suddenly be part of a family that includes several brothers and sisters. Three brothers may have to get used to the idea of having girls in the house. Positions shift as living arrangements change or older kids move on to college or their own apartments. Kids may or may not come to regard stepsiblings as brothers or sisters, depending on such factors as their ages and whether they live in the same house. In our family, for example, Loren never really became a big brother to Peter and Amy because he moved out of our household before they had formed much of a bond. Had we all continued to live together, they would most likely have become closer.

Kids' roles in a stepfamily often need to change in relation to their parents, as well. In a single-parent family, the parent/child roles tend to blur together. Kids may know more about their parents' lives and be more involved in decision-making than they would be in a two-parent household. When the parent remarries, there is a new partner to share the responsibilities, so the kids are expected to go back to being kids. This can be tough for everybody. The kids don't want to give up the closeness they have had with their parent, and they don't appreciate what feels like a loss of importance in the family. Those feelings, of course, tend to come out as resentment toward the stepparent.

You as a parent and stepparent can't really do a great deal to fix conflicts and chaos based on changing roles. What you can do is expect them to happen, so at least you can handle them with more understanding and compassion. The key word here—as usual—is "flexibility." Don't figure out each kid's role, put them into a box with the appropriate label, and expect them to stay there. Instead, do your best to deal with each person in the family the way they are at a particular time. Let kids work out their own relationships with one another as they grow. And keep reminding yourself that the only thing you can count on is change.

"Stepparent" is Not a Dirty Word

When Loren was selected "student of the month" in eighth grade, our local newspaper listed him as "the son of Dean Fox and Kathleen Turner."

Dean, who tends to drool whenever he watches a Kathleen Turner movie, thought the notice was funny. If Ms. Turner had a problem with suddenly becoming the mother of a teenager, she didn't let us know about it. I was jointly amused and annoyed but, figuring hardly anyone would read the fine print of the school news anyway, didn't care very much. And Loren's father was irate. Understandably, he didn't appreciate one bit being completely omitted from the notice of his son's accomplishment.

Most of the problem came from the family information sheets the students completed in school at the beginning of the year. The forms, created in times when families were more strictly defined, didn't have spaces to list stepfathers or stepmothers or any other "unconventional" living arrangements.

Filling out the form as best he could, Loren put his stepfather down as "head of household," put me down as "other parent," and didn't find room anywhere for his dad. (We never did figure out how Kathleen Turner got in there, except possibly through the fantasy of a typesetter at the newspaper.)

This was a relatively small incident, but it's typical of the way stepfamilies fall through the bureaucratic cracks. Even though there are so many of us, we usually aren't officially noticed. Even the agencies which acknowledge that parents do divorce usually assume the children live with one parent or the other. They don't have room in their databases for kids like Dean's, who live half the year with us and half the year with their mother.

The forms we fill out at the school or the doctor's office or the dentist's office don't have space for two family addresses. Yet it's important for those offices to have that information.

Compared with the other stresses and complications that are part of being a blended family, this is a minor irritation. But because it's an inconvenience, I sometimes choose to make an issue of it anyway. So I squawk—in a nice way, of course. First I squeeze in both addresses, the dates the kids live at each house, and the names of all the parents and stepparents, whether there's space for them on the form or not. Then I let someone know how helpful it would be if they considered changing their documents.

It isn't necessary to be obnoxious about this. Yelling at a receptionist who had nothing to do with designing the forms and has no power to change them doesn't accomplish anything. A polite letter to a school principal or someone else who does have some authority is much more constructive.

Don't be shy about asking schools to provide duplicate copies of report cards, to send mail to both families, and to set up two sets of parent conferences if necessary. They are usually more than willing to be cooperative in getting information to both families. After all, even if the district's forms haven't always kept up with reality, teachers and administrators are fully aware of the hassles of stepfamilying. Since one of the school's goals is getting parents to be more involved, staff members are likely to go out of their way to help when they have two sets of parents who do want to know what's going on.

Medical records are sometimes more difficult. Part of the problem is that, in most states, a stepparent has no real legal status when it comes to stepchildren. You may not even be legally qualified to authorize medical treatment.

Our family has handled this situation with a "go ahead and sign it anyway" approach. I have regularly signed school permission slips, medical consent forms, and other authorizations for my stepkids, and I've never had anyone question my right to do so. Dean has done the same for my kids. When Stephanie sprained her ankle a couple years ago, both her mother and Dean happened to be out of town. Someone from the emergency room called me to come down and authorize treatment for her, knowing full well that I was her stepmother and that she didn't live with me. I'm not sure whether they didn't know of my questionable legal status or whether they figured a present unauthorized adult was better than an absent authorized one.

While it has worked for us, this rather casual approach might not be the best way to handle things, especially if you have kids with chronic health problems or if you need to deal with large medical bureaucracies. Some families handle this problem by having a power of attorney or similar document which gives the stepparent authority if the biological parent isn't available. It might well be worthwhile to check out the specifics of the law in your state and have such a form completed just in case you need it.

It's easy to write yourself into the margins of a school form or tell a medical clerk you belong in the emergency room with your stepchild. None of that is personal. It gets harder to make sure you're included when stepchildren, former spouses, or even your spouse don't think you should be.

Sometimes the solution is to get a little pushy. My friend Arnie and his second wife Marta, several years after their marriage, used this approach at his daughter's wedding. His daughter didn't want Marta in any of the wedding pictures. Arnie's position was that she was his wife and, if she weren't included in the photos, he wasn't going to be in them, either. The two of them, agreeing that this issue was important enough to fight for, went to the wedding determined to be pleasant and friendly but to stand their ground about the pictures. Arnie's daughter included Marta in the pictures and, ironically, the previously distant relationship between stepmother and stepdaughter began to improve from that time on.

Pushing your way in isn't always the right thing to do, though. Suppose in this same situation, Arnie had just recently left his first wife in order to marry Marta. Then the daughter's resentment would have been far more understandable, and for Marta to insist on being included in the pictures would have been obnoxious. In fact, her presence at the wedding would probably have been inappropriate. She would have had to move much more slowly, allowing time for wounds to heal, before she could expect to make a place for herself and begin to be accepted by Arnie's children.

Or what if Marta had felt she belonged in the family photos, but Arnie, trying to keep his daughter happy and his ex-wife calm, hadn't backed her up? Then her choices would have been to give in as gracefully as possible or to try to convince Arnie that this issue was important to her.

As you work on making a place for yourself in the family, it's important to choose your battles. Some issues just simply aren't worth fussing over. Make sure of your spouse's support first if you do decide you need to fight to be included in some particular event. It's also essential to use your compassion, your understanding, and your common sense. Just because you belong at your stepson's basketball games, for example, doesn't mean you have to park yourself right behind the coach and bellow advice. Just because you have a right to participate in your stepdaughter's wedding doesn't mean you should expect to be treated in exactly the same way as the mother of the bride. Do your best to understand the needs and feelings of other family members and work your way in tactfully.

As long as you're being considerate and respectful of other family members' needs, a useful strategy is to assume you're invited unless you specifically aren't. Because if you wait to be asked to family events, school conferences, or soccer games, you might wait for a long time. Your spouse may either assume you are included, assume you don't want to be bothered, or simply not think to invite you. Your spouse's ex might well think you don't belong. Your stepkids may resent your presence, especially at first. They are likely to welcome and appreciate it eventually, though even then they probably won't say anything. So don't hold your breath waiting to be welcomed. Just show up. Smile. Applaud. (Without making an exhibition of yourself, of course.) Act as if you belong, and sooner or later you will.

Don't be afraid to introduce yourself as "Mary's stepfather," either. Some people don't like the term "stepparent" because they believe it has so many negative connotations. Which of course it does, especially if you remember your fairy tales and all those wicked stepmothers. In her book *The Combined Family*, Taube Kaufman has even gone so far as to invent completely new terms for members of a stepfamily. To me, this is going about things backwards. What we need is not to change the words, but to change the connotations.

There's nothing wrong with being a stepmother or stepfather. If we hesitate to introduce ourselves as such, we're letting ourselves be controlled by folk tales that are generations old. After all, I'm not Cinderella or Snow White's stepmother—I'm Stephanie and Amy and Peter's stepmother. And that's a perfectly okay role to have.

According to figures from the Stepfamily Association of America, one-fifth of all married-couple households with children are stepfamilies. We are not oddities or rare exceptions to the rule. Yet much of society continues to regard us that way. As long as we tolerate that attitude, it's what we will get. All of us can, politely but firmly, insist upon being acknowledged in small ways. Our doing so will help the blended family be recognized in larger ways as a legitimate family structure which needs and deserves recognition and support.

Four

Pollyanna Had a Point;
Focusing on the Positives

Stepparenting With an Attitude

The first winter that we had all the kids living at our house, Dean was telling a woman at his office about being a stepfather. "Yeah, I think I'm really a great guy, the way I put up with Kathleen's three stepkids." She was amazed. "But if you have three kids, and she has two, and then she has three stepkids—that's eight kids!" About that time the grin on his face gave her a clue, and she figured out that my three stepkids were the same as his three kids. He and I have made a joke ever since of how wonderful we are to put up with each other's stepkids.

But your attitude toward your spouse's kids is no joking matter. A stepparent's underlying attitude toward the partner's children is an important factor in the success or failure of the blended family. Do you think of them as burdens to be endured? As blessings to be loved? As little monsters deliberately out to make your life hell? As adorable but badly reared children who only need your loving hand to improve their lives?

The two extreme points of view toward stepchildren are acute resentment and jealousy on one hand and trying to adopt them on the other. Position A might be something like this: "I've made it clear to George that I don't intend to put up with his rotten kids any more than I have to. I'll be so glad when they're grown up and out of our lives so I don't have to deal with them any more." Position B would be more like this: "Sometimes I wish George's ex-wife would die or run off to Tahiti or something so we could have the kids all the time. I love them so much I wish we didn't have to share them with her."

These extremes have one important characteristic in common. They both are fantasy. If you resent your stepkids, you're kidding yourself if you think you can ignore them even after they grow up. If you wish you were the kids' real parent, you are denying the reality that the job has already been filled by someone who comes far ahead of you in their hearts. And both extremes are harmful. If you resent your stepkids, you're wronging both the children and your spouse by pushing them away from one another. If you try to take the kids away emotionally from their other parent, you are confusing them and setting yourself up for heartache.

The attitude of most stepparents, of course, falls somewhere in between. And it may vary from time to time. But going into the stepfamily with an intent to accept your stepchildren as the real, complicated people they are is a good place to start. Each child will come into the stepfamily with an individual history and a unique combination of pain, resentment, jealousy, and fear—possibly mixed with some curiosity and willingness to be friendly. All of that is part of the package that your spouse brought to this marriage. Meeting the kids more than halfway with an attitude of realistic acceptance is a first step toward building a healthy stepfamily.

Realistic acceptance involves a lot more than facing the fact that this stepfamilying is going to be tough. Part of it is admitting that things are a lot less than perfect. But the other part of it is honestly acknowledging the good stuff as well as the bad—and the wise stepparent will choose to emphasize the good.

One of the indispensable items I'd put in a toolkit for a new blended family would be a copy of *Pollyanna*, by Eleanor H. Porter. You know who Pollyanna is—she's that mindlessly cheerful child who is so incorrigibly **glad**, even in the face of hardship, that any normal person wants to strangle her. Her name has become a synonym for exaggerated optimism.

41

Well, I went back and re-read *Pollyanna* not long ago, and you know what? This girl's optimism is far from mindless. She's a tough little kid who has been trained by her minister father to look for the good in every situation, and she hangs onto that teaching even in some difficult circumstances. (Although when she loses the use of her legs in an accident, she is initially as depressed and grief-stricken as anyone else would be.) The "glad game" taught by Pollyanna's father makes a challenge out of finding something to be happy about in any situation. One example she describes is when her father's struggling church in a small pioneer town receives a "missionary barrel" of hand-me-downs from the East. Pollyanna, hoping there might be a doll in the barrel, is disappointed to find a pair of crutches instead. So what is there to be glad about in that? After some thinking, she finds it—the fact that she doesn't need the crutches.

I would seriously recommend reading *Pollyanna.* It may be a bit sentimental for our tough-minded times, but it's an excellent book. Or if you just don't think you can handle that much gladness, try *The Power of Positive Thinking,* by Norman Vincent Peale, or *The Road Less Traveled,* by M. Scott Peck. Try anything that will help you focus your attention on the good things in your stepfamily situation.

By positive thinking, I absolutely do not mean putting on a big fake smile and saying through your gritted teeth, "Oh, everything is wonderful." I don't mean a false optimism that is nothing more than denial of reality (like the wife of a still-drinking alcoholic who kept telling her support group, "I'm going to have a good marriage even if I have to do it all by myself."). Or I don't mean what my husband calls "lightworking." This is a particularly New Age twist on optimism which insists that all we need to do to have a perfect world is ignore anything negative and spread around enough love, light, and understanding. Concentrating on the good stuff does not mean never getting angry, never feeling hurt, never having conflicts, or always being happy. It simply means that you choose to emphasize what is good about your situation instead of what is bad about it.

Some people seem to have the ability to do this naturally. There's the story of the little boy who was always such an optimist that his parents decided it was time to teach him some of the cold, hard facts of life. So for his birthday they filled the playhouse in the back yard with manure. They told him where his present was, waited a few minutes, and then followed him out to the yard, ready to explain some realities. When they peeked in the window, there he was, shoveling like mad. "Oh, boy!" he shouted when he saw them. "With all this manure, there just has to be a pony in here somewhere!"

A good many of us aren't born with that much optimism. Even if someone should give us a pony, we're likely to concentrate on the fact that something has to be done with the manure. But even if your natural tendency is to get bogged down in the shoveling, you can still learn to pay more attention to the positives. Maybe you won't become a raving optimist overnight, but with some practice it's possible to strengthen your focus on the good things.

Thank You For Volunteering

The first and most crucial step in becoming more optimistic is to keep in mind that you are a volunteer here, not a victim. Being a victim has its payoffs, of course. Otherwise, why would any of us choose that role? If you are the poor, abused stepparent who has to put up with terrible stepchildren and horrible ex-spouses, you get to be the center of sympathetic attention. A therapist friend of mine called this the "poor Edith, isn't she wonderful?" syndrome, after a woman in his home town who was noted for her long-suffering endurance of abusive treatment by her alcoholic husband.

Sometimes it seems easier to be a "poor Edith" than to acknowledge the positives and work toward making your situation

43

better. However, the victim role isn't a whole lot of fun, and eventually it gets horribly dreary. Your chances for a successful, happy stepfamily are greatly increased by deciding not to see yourself as a victim.

Because the truth is that, as a parent or stepparent, you volunteered. No one held a shotgun to your head as you said "I do" to becoming part of a stepfamily. You may have volunteered in ignorance or innocence, with no real idea of what you were getting into, but you still volunteered. You are part of this family by choice. You have the option of leaving at any time. Since you're reading this, presumably you are planning to stay where you are. In that case, you might as well get all the positives you can out of the situation.

Being a volunteer certainly doesn't mean you have chosen or approve of every part of your family situation. You probably wouldn't choose to have kids and stepkids dislike one another, stepchildren resent you, children live apart from you, or ex-spouses only communicate with you through an attorney. Part of the stress of living in a stepfamily comes from the many aspects of it which are completely beyond your control. But even though you don't have the power to choose those specific elements, always remember that the bottom line is still a matter of your volunteering. You have decided to involve yourself in a stepfamily, which means you have chosen to live with all those situations over which you have no control.

Just because you volunteered doesn't mean you have to accept everything the way it is, of course. In fact, doing your best to improve the family situation is part of your job as a parent and stepparent. But you accomplish those changes far more effectively when you approach them from the perspective of a volunteer, not a victim.

Practice Specific Changes

Becoming more aware of the positives in your stepfamily means taking action. A good first step is simply to acknowledge that there are good things. Some days there aren't many. Some days the closest you might come to finding anything positive is a halfhearted, "Well, I guess it could be worse."

So start there. After all, you're right—it certainly could be worse. If you have trouble finding things to appreciate about your family situation, maybe it would help to start with a list of all the things that could be really bad but aren't.

Maybe everyone is physically healthy. Maybe your alcoholic ex-spouse is still drinking, but at least you aren't living with the addiction every day. Maybe your child's choosing not to live with you means your ex-spouse is getting a chance to be an active parent. Maybe the stepchild who doesn't like you is a good brother or sister to the other kids. Maybe nobody's in trouble with the law or using drugs or flunking out of school. Maybe the roof doesn't leak and the bills are getting paid. Maybe the cat is still around. (Or, depending on your point of view, maybe the cat just ran away.)

Becoming more positive about your stepfamily doesn't happen overnight. You don't just wake up one morning, smile grimly through your toothpaste, and decide you will look on the bright side from now on. You have to practice changing your thinking and your point of view. You might want to try some of these ideas to help shift your thoughts into more optimistic channels:

1. Make periodic lists of the good stuff. Do this in your head or actually sit down and write them out. Include little things as well as big ones, from the fact that your spouse loves you or that you like your job to the way your surly stepson takes quick showers in the mornings so there is less fighting over the bathroom. One exercise that can be fun is to go through the

alphabet and find something starting with each letter which you are grateful for.

2. Practice courtesy. A pleasant tone of voice, "please," and "thank you" are lubricants which help reduce friction. They are also contagious.

3. Praise everyone in your family, especially the most difficult members, whenever you honestly can.

4. Say good things to others about your stepkids or your spouse's ex whenever you have a chance. Don't let all your conversation about them be whining or complaining.

5. Take care of yourself in basic ways, like getting enough sleep and exercising, so you have enough energy to deal with the challenges of your family.

6. Practice putting yourself in the other person's place. Build compassion for your pain-in-the neck stepkids or your inconsiderate former spouse by imagining the feelings that push them to act the way they do. How would you act if you were in their position? (Of course, we all know you would act in a much more mature and courteous manner than they do—but try it anyway just for the challenge.)

7. Find a support group that is a safe place to express your frustrations. This doesn't have to be specifically a stepfamily group. It might be a few friends you go to lunch with now and then, a twelve-step group, a church group, or a therapy group. The important thing is that you have a place where you are expected to share honestly and where confidences will be respected.

8. Try Pollyanna's "glad game"—it really is useful. For example, Rachel recently broke her ankle when she was jumping on our trampoline. These are a few of the things she and I came up with to be glad about: She didn't break her back or her neck; the injury happened to her rather than to one of the neighbor's kids, so nobody sued us; we had good health insurance; my flexible work schedule meant taking her back and forth to school wasn't a problem; after the first few days her leg didn't hurt. There was more, but you get the idea. It helped us keep the proper

perspective and remember that a broken ankle was an inconvenience, not a tragedy.

9. Don't make yourself into a martyr. You are the adult here; your job is to be responsible and mature as you help your kids and stepkids learn to live comfortably together. You can do that job better and maintain your sanity if you practice regular small indulgences that are important to you. This might be an occasional bubble bath, a special stash of chocolate that you don't share (my personal favorite), time alone with a good book, or whatever works for you. Being a parent and stepparent realistically demands sacrifice, effort, and delayed gratification. The big sacrifices are easier to make if you allow yourself some small luxuries along the way.

10. Create a mental album or shoebox of good memories, big and little. Take them out and look at them every now and then to remind yourself that they are a part of stepfamilying just as much as the stresses and problems. Some of mine are:

•Finding two first-grade drawings of hearts taped to the wall in my room, one reading, "I love Mom," and the other reading, "I love Kathleen."

•Getting to go to holiday programs with my husband at three different schools.

•Sitting at the supper table with five kids who are all trying to see how far they can cross their eyes.

•Listening to two or three of the kids negotiate their way through the question of whether someone is hogging the computer and who gets to play on it next and what would be a fair way to take turns—and staying out of it.

•Having Peter, at age five, tell me wistfully, "I wish things were like they used to be and I just lived in one house and had one Mom." But having him add with impeccable grace and tact, "Then my Mom would be my Mom and you would still be my friend."

Don't Waste Your Energy on Fantasy

Loren graduated from high school a few years ago. I had a great time at the graduation ceremony; I had a terrible time the week before. It wasn't because anything awful happened. It was because I spent several days in fury and frustration wishing for "what could be." Trying to reconcile fantasy and reality left me feeling sad, angry, and resentful.

The fantasy went something like this: The whole family—Dean and I, my kids, his kids, and assorted relatives—would get together for a graduation party. Loren's father would be welcome if he wanted to come. Everyone would get along comfortably. Loren would let us know how grateful he was for everything we had done for him. We'd all fade out at the end in a rosy glow of family warmth and togetherness.

The reality was more like this: Loren and his stepfather had hardly spoken since Loren moved out over two years earlier, and neither of them would be comfortable at a family gathering with the other. Having family there for his graduation meant a lot to Loren. Some of my relatives were coming, but I wouldn't know till the last minute how many. It was very important to Rachel to spend time celebrating her brother's graduation. Dean's kids didn't care much one way or another—Stephanie was working that day and Peter and Amy mostly wanted to know if "party" meant "cake and ice cream." Loren's dad wasn't interested in any kind of cooperative celebration.

And I was furious about all that. I wanted everyone to like each other. I wanted some family togetherness and celebration for this occasion. I wanted us to be a perfect family.

After all my inner whining and wishing, this is the way we spent the day: Dean took himself out of a potentially awkward situation and did something he wanted to do by taking Peter and

Amy fishing. Rachel and I picked Loren up at his dad's house and brought him home for dinner. My mother, aunt, and two sisters came, bringing gifts and cookies. We didn't have an elaborate party, but spent the afternoon visiting and munching. Stephanie got off work just in time to go to graduation with us.

The ceremony was well-organized and mercifully brief. Loren was one of the four commencement speakers and by far the best (in our unbiased opinions). Afterward, his father visited briefly with my family. Loren collected his congratulations with thanks, hugged everybody, and left for a party with his friends. The rest of us went home and ordered pizza, since the fishermen hadn't caught anything.

And it was a good day. It wasn't perfect, if "perfect" means everyone together in one big happy family. But it was an appropriate recognition of this milestone in Loren's life. We got through what could have been a difficult time with laughter, grace, and chocolate chip cookies.

The fantasy would have been wonderful to have. But the reality was what we did have, and it also had a great deal of good in it. When I started paying attention to that good instead of wasting energy on the fantasy, most of my pain and anger went away.

It is crucial in stepfamilies that we learn to live in reality instead of fantasy. Our families aren't going to be just the way we wish they could be. Our celebrations aren't going to be perfect Norman Rockwell occasions. (By the way, it may help to consider that they probably weren't perfect in Norman Rockwell's family, either.)

Whether you are dealing with celebrations and milestones or just the day-to-day realities of living together, developing a more positive attitude about your stepfamily means first of all accepting the facts of your particular situation. You don't live in the Brady family, or your sister-in-law's friend Shirley's family, or the family down the block. You live in your family, whatever it may be like.

Don't compare your situation to someone else's. It may appear to you that other stepfamilies are doing better than yours—that the kids don't fight as much, the ex-spouses are more cooperative, or the parents manage more effectively. That may be true. Or it may not. You have no way of knowing, because all you see of that other family is the outside. If you measure your own situation against theirs, you are comparing your family's inside with the other family's outside, which doesn't give you any useful information at all.

If you know someone whose stepfamily appears to do well, by all means get to know them better. You might learn some valuable things about coping strategies or parenting skills. But don't waste time wishing your family were like theirs. If you want to change the way your family functions, that's wonderful—but you can only do so by starting with the reality of the way it functions now. If your ex-spouse is a drug addict who lives three states away and never sees the kids, that is a fact you need to deal with. If your teenage stepdaughter resents you and never opens her mouth except to say something sarcastic, that is the reality which is the starting point if you want to build a better relationship with her.

Accepting the reality of your family situation certainly doesn't mean giving up any attempts to improve it. But you can't change anything unless you first acknowledge the way it really is. Staying in fantasy does nothing but build up resentment and frustration over what you wish for but don't have. When you accept reality instead, you acknowledge both the good and the bad about what you do have. Then you can start to build on what is good and change what isn't. If you want to create a strong family unit, reality is the only solid foundation on which to build it.

Wisdom to Know What You Can Change

Once you accept the reality of your particular stepfamily, then you can go on to consider which parts of that reality can be changed and which cannot. A useful tool is the following:

> God grant me the serenity
> To accept the things I cannot change,
> Courage to change the things I can,
> And wisdom to know the difference.

This Serenity Prayer, adapted from a prayer originally written by Reinhold Niebuhr, is used widely in twelve-step programs. It is a valuable piece of wisdom to apply to stepfamilying, both for the success of your blended family and for your own piece of mind.

Think for a minute about the things in your stepfamily that you cannot change. Some of them might be: the presence of former spouses as part of your children's lives, the fact that living conditions are chaotic as kids move in and out, the fact that your stepchildren love their real mother or father more than they will ever love you, the fact that you have no control over living conditions or rules at the other parent's house, or the fact that you cannot force stepsiblings to like each other.

And what about the things you can change? These might include: your attitude toward your stepchildren or former spouses, your parenting skills, the house or neighborhood in which you live, conflict between you and your spouse about money or discipline, or the amount of time you commit to your job or other activities.

Obviously the specifics of what can or cannot be changed will depend on your exact circumstances. You may find it useful to make a mental list that fits your own stepfamily. If you do, keep in mind that your list won't necessarily be limited to things you can *easily* change. The word "courage" isn't in there by accident. It's easier to complain to your spouse about your stepson's bullying of your daughter than to initiate a family meeting to talk about the problem. It's easier to see yourself as a victim than to stand up for yourself and set boundaries. It's easier to avoid a sullen stepdaughter than to take steps to get to know her.

Remember, too, that just because something can be changed doesn't always mean it should be changed. Taking your former spouse to court to get sole custody of a child, for example, might be possible, but might not necessarily be the best thing for the child. Or you might have the legal authority to force a child to live with you when they would rather be with their other parent, but that doesn't mean it would be a good idea to insist.

This is where the "wisdom to the know the difference" part comes in. And it often adds up to this: the most important thing you can change in any situation—and sometimes the only thing you have the power to change—is your own attitude. While you can set and enforce boundaries about other people's behavior, you cannot force them to alter their feelings. You certainly can effect changes in your blended family, but only by starting with yourself.

In our stepfamily, one of the biggest sources of conflict at the beginning was a power struggle between Loren and Stephanie. Loren, at 13 with one little sister who thought he was terrific, didn't take being the oldest too seriously but wasn't about to give up the prestige of the position. Stephanie, also the oldest in her family, was a bossy 10-year-old who was used to running everything for Peter and Amy. She wasn't about to step aside for any mere boy just because he was three years older. The battle was joined. Loren was older and stronger, but Stephanie was at that time a more skilled warrior. Her specialty was to bait Loren in subtle ways until she goaded him into blatant retaliation, which of course got him into trouble and left her in the position of the innocent victim. The conflict was exacerbated by the fact that the younger kids felt obligated to take sides.

Obviously, this was a situation that needed to be changed if at all possible. So, applying the Serenity Prayer, what would have been some of my options? (I didn't do this at the time, by the way—it would have been helpful if I had.) What I couldn't change included their feelings about each other, their basic personalities, their ages, or their ways of behaving.

So what could I change? Let's start with the drastic options first. I could have taken my kids and moved out. I could have issued an ultimatum to Dean, telling him I refused to live with his horrible oldest child and pushing him to choose between us. I could have isolated both kids to their rooms except for mealtimes and school. I could have given up in despair and done nothing, letting the two of them fight it out.

Some of these choices, of course, would have been ridiculously out of proportion to the problem, and none of them would have been particularly constructive. Fortunately, these weren't any of the responses I chose at the time.

What Dean and I did was set limits on their behavior by imposing consequences for name-calling, invading each other's rooms, or hitting each other. I tried to assign chores and plan activities in ways to break up the "Dean's kids vs. Kathleen's kids" units so the younger kids would be less involved in the conflict. I did my best to listen to both Loren and Stephanie and arbitrate disputes as fairly as possible. (My yardstick for success in this was, "If both of them think I'm being unfair, then I'm probably on the right track.") Dean and I discussed the problem so we could do our best to respond to it with a united front. I also spent more than a few sleepless nights, shed more than a few tears, and lost my temper more than once.

Eventually, as everyone got used to living together, both Loren and Stephanie eased back on the power struggle and began to co-exist with less friction. The conflict wasn't ever completely resolved, though. It eventually ended when, during our third year as a stepfamily, Loren went to live with his father and Stephanie promptly and firmly picked up the reins as the oldest kid.

For me to have applied the Serenity Prayer in this situation would have saved some wear and tear on all of us. First of all, I could have changed my attitude. As Loren's mother, I naturally tended to assume he was always right, especially considering the fact that I was having my own power struggles with Stephanie at the time. I could have changed that point of view and tried to look at their various encounters more objectively. I could have changed the way I thought of Stephanie—paying more attention to the vulnerability and fear that were behind her attempts to be in control and run the whole household. I could have reminded myself that they were both children and therefore not really as powerful as they sometimes seemed. With this change in attitude as a foundation, I would most likely have been able to help resolve the conflict more effectively. My actual responses to the situation wouldn't have changed a great deal, but the attitude behind them would have been more relaxed. I don't know how much difference this would have made to Loren and Stephanie, but it certainly would have spared me some stomachaches and sleepless nights.

Five

Learning to Live with Built-In Chaos

Life in a healthy traditional family might be compared to living in a house built on good solid ground. We know what's under us and (unless we live along the San Andreas Fault) it stays put. A stepfamily is more like living on a houseboat. The deck beneath our feet keeps shifting and rolling. About the time we think we have its rhythm figured out, the wind changes or a storm comes up, and we're tossed off balance again.

That shifting foundation is a fact of life in a blended family. Family traditions and styles aren't as deeply ingrained. Stepsiblings are part of different extended families. Living arrangements are likely to change as kids get older or parents relocate or remarry. It's a pointless and losing battle to try to make the foundation stay still. Instead, you need to learn to live with the chaos and accommodate to the constant changes.

The Magic Word is "Flexible"

An essential quality for thriving in a stepfamily is *flexibility*. Recite it as a mantra before you go to sleep at night. Engrave it on your keychain or tattoo it on your forehead. There are times when you will need to know your bottom line and stand firmly by it; we'll discuss that subject more fully in a later chapter. But on everything except the serious bottom-line issues, flexibility is essential both for your sanity and the survival of your stepfamily.

Seeing the wisdom of this and practicing it are two different things. You simply cannot realize how set in your ways you are until you become part of a stepfamily. Along the way all of us develop personal and family habits and traditions, which govern everything from the best make of car to drive to the right way to peel potatoes. (I use a paring knife; my husband uses a vegetable peeler—which to me is a carrot peeler because that's the only thing I use it for.)

While you and your kids have been learning one "right" set of habits, of course, your spouse and stepkids have been learning another. The two are bound to clash—sometimes loudly. Then add in the need to accommodate custody and visitation schedules, kids spending time in more than one household, and all the other moving parts that make up stepfamilies. In the middle of all that chaos, clinging rigidly to your own way of doing things may seem like a way to preserve some order and sanity. It isn't. Instead, it will only add to the stress for everyone. It's a far saner choice to be as flexible as you can, both within your own stepfamily and in dealing with ex-spouses and children's other families.

Now, I am not inherently a flexible person. I like my routines to follow along in their appointed paths. I like to find my toothpaste and my hairbrush where I left them. I find it annoying when someone installs games on my computer without asking me first. I like things done the right way (which is usually my way, of course). So learning the flexibility that's necessary to be comfortable in a stepfamily hasn't been easy for me. I'm sure, actually, that my stepkids would be quick to tell you I still haven't learned it.

So how do you learn to be more flexible? The same way you learn most things—trial and error, plus a lot of practice. Here are some strategies that have been helpful for me:

1. Practice changing your thinking to open yourself up to more options. Instead of having a mindset of "this is the way this is supposed to be done," try something like "this is the way that works best for me." Your habits and patterns are just that—habits.

They weren't engraved on stone tablets by God and handed to you on top of a mountain. Just because something works well for you doesn't necessarily mean it is the only choice available.

2. Remind yourself that it's okay for the procedure to be different as long as the job gets done. Maybe you always wash the towels in cold water, and your stepdaughter has been taught to use warm. As long as the laundry gets done, who on earth cares?

3. Decide which is more important, being happy or getting your own way. (And no, the two aren't necessarily synonymous.)

4. Think about why you do something a certain way. Is it because experience has taught you that it works best? Fine—then explain your reasons to the rest of the family in a way that might convert them to your way of thinking. Is it out of habit? Then maybe there are other choices that might be just as effective.

5. Keep your sense of humor. A light touch works wonders. I serve toasted cheese sandwiches and make dressing with turkey; my stepkids were raised to eat grilled cheese sandwiches and stuffing. We've made these into jokes that pop up almost every time one of those foods appears on the table.

6. Use the Serenity Prayer often to help you figure out when to stand your ground and when to give in.

7. Ask yourself, "How important will this be in thirty years? Or thirty days? Or even thirty minutes?"

8. Remind yourself that chaos and complications are part of the package that you chose to accept in becoming part of a stepfamily. This is not personal. You simply aren't going to get your way all the time—or even most of the time. Needing to become more flexible doesn't imply a criticism of your character or mean you've done anything wrong up to this point; it's just part of the job description for being a good stepparent.

9. Remember that taking the high road means you will always come out on top. Be the first to be flexible about holiday schedules, time with the kids' other families, etc. Your willingness to accommodate and adjust will make life smoother for everyone in the family, including yourself. And who knows—you might

even get some appreciation once in a while for being easy to get along with. (Please don't count on the appreciation, though, or you're likely to be disappointed. Be flexible because it's the best thing to do, not because you expect someone to thank you for it.)

10. You don't have to give up everything you're used to doing. It's reasonable to expect others in the stepfamily to be flexible, too. If you're the only one adapting and compromising, you're being stepped on, which is probably going to result in your building up a lot of resentment that will go off and hurt somebody someday. This doesn't mean it's okay for you to be rigid just for the sake of having your own way. Nor do you have the right to take advantage of someone else's flexibility. But keep in mind that the goal is to take something from everyone, compromise, adapt, and develop new habits and traditions that work well for the whole blended family.

11. Don't confuse flexibility with being victimized. It is not a synonym for "letting yourself be taken advantage of." You don't have to be a wimp or a doormat. Think of yourself as being graciously accommodating from a position of strength, rather than as losing a power struggle or being taken advantage of. Then you can rearrange your schedule or give up your plans without feeling resentful.

12. Make a mental poster that says, "so what?" So what if the rules are different at the kids' other household than they are at yours? The kids will learn to adapt. So what if Christmas gets celebrated at your house on December 26? The important thing is the observance, not the date. So what if the kids want to go on a camping trip with Dad and it isn't his usual weekend with them? Rearrange the schedule and let them go camping. Life is too short to spend it being rigid and getting angry every time you have to change your plans.

Where's the Harm?

An important skill for succeeding in a stepfamily is learning to choose your battles wisely. (General Custer probably isn't your best role model here.) Some things are worth fighting over, and some things aren't. Your challenge is to figure out when to charge and when to withdraw gracefully.

Back in the days when I judged high school debates, I learned a phrase that's been useful in this area. It wasn't enough for the debaters to present an alternative to the current situation; they had to demonstrate that the status quo had flaws which would be repaired by their proposed change. If they didn't do so, the opposing team would attack: "Where's the harm? They haven't shown us the harm in the status quo."

Before getting into a power struggle or rising to a challenge, it often helps to stop and ask yourself, "Where's the harm here?" Is anybody going to get hurt, has a household rule been broken, is my authority being questioned in such a way that I need to assert it?

Sometimes the answer is yes, sometimes no. But asking the question helps get your feelings out of the way long enough to look at a situation objectively. Then you can deal with it based on the facts. As stepparents, it's easy to react to personalities or your own feelings more than situations. A disagreement or a simple matter of discipline can get mixed up with your own stuff about who is right or wrong and who is really in charge. Asking "Where's the harm?" helps keep those issues in perspective so you can focus on the question at hand.

After you've established "Where's the harm," the next logical question is, "How much harm?" Is this issue important enough to take a stand on? Is it worth the energy you or another family member are giving it? Just how big a deal is this?

A counselor I used to work with had two guidelines for dealing with life's crises:

1. Don't sweat the small stuff.

2. Everything short of a life-threatening situation is small stuff.

These are excellent and inspiring guidelines. They would have been even more inspiring if she had actually practiced them. (This same woman once called me from 2,000 miles away at 6:00 a.m., in a panic because the airline had lost her luggage and I was supposed to keep calling them every half hour until it turned up.)

"Don't sweat the small stuff" doesn't necessarily mean enduring every little annoyance. That too often can result in resenting small things until they grow into big things. Instead, it means comfortably ignoring things that don't really matter, but taking care of the small stuff which does matter in a small way as it happens. So perhaps better advice would be "don't sweat the small stuff—but do deal with it so it doesn't grow into big stuff." If small stuff is allowed to pile up, gathering resentment along the way, it eventually becomes big stuff which explodes unexpectedly in someone's face.

It's the small stuff, after all, which makes up the fabric of our day-to-day lives. And it's that same stuff which cause a disproportionate amount of stress in a blended family. It isn't our fellow family members' philosophies of life or career choices that make us decide we can't possibly survive one more day in the same household. It's the way they constantly borrow our tools without returning them or leave dirty socks on the floor or turn the TV up too loud.

A lot of small stuff isn't worth bothering about. Some of it is important. The tricky part is figuring out which is which. The Serenity Prayer is useful here. So is remembering to figure out "where's the harm." I also have a rule of thumb that says if it makes my stomach hurt or keeps me awake, I need to deal with it; if I can forget about it in half an hour, it doesn't matter.

As we try to keep the friction in a stepfamily at a manageable level, it's often the small stuff that needs attention. It's silly to waste energy on trivial issues. It's inappropriate to over-react with punishments or screaming to minor irritations. But it's useful and tension-easing to politely but clearly ask someone to pick up after themselves or leave your things alone or turn down the TV.

And it's just as important to respect other people's stuff, which may seem small to you but be important to them. Maybe you think it's trivial that your four-year-old son tore up the play money from his teenage stepbrother's Monopoly game. To your stepson, that might well be a serious violation of his property rights. Your job as the parent and stepparent here would be to keep the older boy from mangling the little one, but also to replace the money and impose some consequences on the four-year-old. In the process, you would be striking a small blow for justice as well as teaching your stepson that you could be trusted to be fair.

So as you practice not sweating the small stuff, remember not to discount it, either—whether it's your own or someone else's. As long as you deal with small stuff so everyone can then forget about it, it won't grow into big stuff that's a big deal to take care of.

What Would Happen If You Didn't?

You've always opened gifts on Christmas morning instead of Christmas Eve. You've always made raking the leaves in the fall a family project. You've always had pancakes for breakfast on Sundays. You've always taken your kids out to dinner on their birthdays. You've always gone camping for a couple weeks every summer. You've always had a big family reunion on the Fourth of July.

Every family has traditions, habits, and styles like these which are simply accepted as "the way we always do that." A divorce can shake up and alter many of those traditions, but most of the time parents make an attempt to hang onto the ones which are important to the kids. When you get involved in a blended family is when it gets really tricky, because sometimes "our" traditions and styles conflict with "theirs."

61

This can result in open battles or silent power struggles as each side of the family tries to defend its turf and hang onto its customs. Or it can lead to resentment and ill-will as some family members feel they are "losing" by giving up what they are used to.

The three best ways to deal with this situation are communication, communication, and communication. Suppose your stepson expects that on his birthday he will get to choose the dinner menu because that's the tradition in his family, but nobody tells you that. You fix an ordinary meal but plan to make a big deal over cake and ice cream later, because that's what your family does. He's likely to be hurt and angry because he feels discounted, and you're likely to be hurt and bewildered because he doesn't appreciate the effort you went to in decorating the cake. Some simple communication goes a long way toward eliminating this kind of stress.

So don't blindly try to follow your own traditions or assume everyone in the new family will happily adopt them. Ask questions. Find out how your stepkids are used to celebrating holidays or how your spouse feels about going camping. Tell them what your family customs are. Sharing this kind of information can be a fun way to learn more about one another, especially if you do it without an attitude of "our way is better than yours."

Talking about traditions and styles can also give you a chance to question why all of you do what you do in the particular ways you do it. Why do you always bake a dozen kinds of cookies at Christmas? Why do you always spend your vacation camping? Why do you believe kids should or shouldn't have phones in their rooms? How important is a particular custom? Do you have to do it that way? What would happen if you didn't?

Asking questions like these can help everyone in the family decide which traditions are really important and which ones don't matter very much. Then as a stepfamily you can build new shared traditions that make sense for all of you.

As you're creating new family traditions, keep a few things in mind:

1. For personal events like birthdays, it's always best to add rather than subtract. Combine customs from both sides of the family as much as you can, so kids don't feel they are losing something.

2. For events such as family reunions on one side of the family, it might be best to make participation optional for stepkids. They don't know all these people, and depending on their ages and how much time they spend in your household, they may never get to know your relatives particularly well. Don't insist that they necessarily get heavily involved with your extended family—but don't give up your own participation, either, if it's important to you.

3. Remember that building new family traditions isn't something you do overnight. Yes, make some deliberate choices and decisions about what customs you want to have. But a tradition is something that evolves over time and gradually becomes meaningful to everyone. Let this happen naturally in your stepfamily.

An example of this in our family is the annual Christmas tree hunt. The first year we were together as a blended family, we decided to cut our own Christmas tree. We live near a national forest where tree-cutting is common, but though Dean and his kids had cut trees before, my kids and I hadn't. It was going to be the start of a special family tradition, part of the ideal family Christmas out of Currier and Ives by way of Norman Rockwell. So we loaded everybody into the Suburban and headed out in search of family bonding and the perfect spruce tree.

It was awful. The first dirt road we tried wound on and on through pines and aspens, with no spruce trees in sight. After a few miles, rebellion broke out in the back seat. "This is stupid." "How come all the fuss over a dumb old tree, anyway?" "Why can't we just go buy a tree?" "Peter is turning green—I think he's going to throw up." "I'm thirsty." "This isn't any fun."

We finally found a different road and a stand of lovely small spruce trees. By then Dean and I were both snarling at the kids that they could just stay home next year. And of course, as soon as we all got out of the car and actually started to look for a tree, the kids had as much fun as if the whole expedition had been their idea in the first place.

The second year, we had all forgotten most of the complaints from the year before, so we went out again. This time, we found spruce trees on our first try. It was a beautiful warm day, more like early September than mid-December. We hiked up a logging road in the sunshine, finding one nice tree, then another, and finally the one which everyone agreed was perfect.

The two oldest kids took turns using the saw, and we started back down the road with the three younger kids carrying the tree. And all at once, as Dean and I followed them, time stopped for me. It was one of those moments that store themselves indelibly in the brain and say, "Remember this instant. This is happiness." For a moment everything was perfect.

Then time started moving again, and we went on to the Suburban and loaded the tree and took it home.

The third year, I was out of town on Christmas-tree cutting weekend. Dean and the kids went with a group of friends, got stuck in a snowbank, and quite unreasonably had a terrific time without me.

The fourth year, we set out with three friends the morning after a snowstorm. We waded through soft waist-high snow, falling down, laughing, and finding our trees by digging for them. Our fun was touched with a special poignancy as we cut an extra tiny tree for a dying friend in the hospital.

Each year since, we have gone to cut a tree. But by now we've given up trying to do it right. To heck with family bonding; we just go get a Christmas tree.

And a funny thing has happened along the way. As we're on our way to the woods, the kids reminisce. Isn't that the place we got stuck that time? Remember how warm it was that one year? Remember when we cut that little tree for Gene? In spite of

64

ourselves, year by year, we have built a tradition that is important to all of us.

Keep Out of My Space and Get Your Mitts Off My Stuff!

Do you know where your hairbrush is? How about your scissors? Do family members routinely interrupt when someone else is talking? Do kids often get into fights about using one another's things or borrowing clothes? Do people at your house knock or just walk in if a bedroom door is closed?

All of these questions have to do with boundaries. Setting boundaries in a family ranges from minor issues like borrowing hairbrushes to major ones like sexual or bathing privacy and protection of private material such as diaries. Especially in stepfamilies, respecting others' boundaries is an important part of living together comfortably. Conflicts arise when the two "sides" of the family have different boundary patterns. It's valuable to establish clear boundaries early in your stepfamilying, which might take some compromise if there are significant differences.

For example, I hate to have anyone borrow my personal stuff. My hairbrush, makeup, art supplies, and stuff on my desk are MINE, and I don't want anyone else using them, even if that person is someone I love. I really see red if the borrower doesn't even ask first or if they don't return something despite solemn promises to do so. My kids both learned that attitude to a degree (although they're a lot more tolerant about borrowing than they are about being borrowed from).

Dean and his kids came into the household with a more casual attitude about using one another's things and walking into one another's rooms. At first we thought they were rude and they thought we were picky. But gradually we all have become comfortable with boundaries that work for us most of the time.

Now, the kids don't even ask any more to use my hairbrush or my colored pencils, because they know I'm unreasonable about it.

They borrow one another's stuff more casually, but are fairly careful about asking first and returning what they borrow. The kids always knock if our bedroom door is shut, and they almost always offer that same courtesy to each other. Dean and I don't go into their rooms without knocking, either.

Whether they are intended to provided privacy for adults or protection for kids, boundaries and limits are crucial in a stepfamily and need to be observed by all the family members. Boundaries are ultimately a matter of respect for one another's person, property, and privacy. Some of the ways to show that respect include:

1. Expecting everyone, adults and children alike, to knock if bedroom doors are closed. This should be an absolute rule for everyone in the family, from adults to toddlers. It's especially important for a couple in a new stepfamily to be clear and firm about this in order to protect their relationship. You need your privacy and some time together. My belief is that your bedroom ought to be your territory, essentially off-limits to kids without an invitation. Other families are more casual about this, with everyone snuggling on the bed sometimes to watch TV or read the Sunday comics. Regardless of your own approach, you certainly need to be available to small children for nighttime emergencies such as nosebleeds or nightmares. But that doesn't mean you need a constant open-door policy.

Single parents with young children often relax bedroom boundaries considerably, so the kids get into the habit of crawling into bed with Mom or Dad. It can be a shock when all of a sudden a new stepparent is occupying that bed and not appreciating company. It's hard for the parent, too, who may feel caught in the middle, wanting to have privacy with the new spouse but not abandon or neglect the child. It seems to me that the best approach here is to set a "no visitors" limit firmly right away and get it over with, rather than vacillating with "just this once will be okay." Depending on the age of the child, you might compensate by spending more time tucking them in, making a fuss over a new bedspread or rearranged bedroom, or getting them a special new stuffed animal to sleep with. Ease your guilt feelings by reminding yourself that keeping kids in their own beds isn't just for the benefit of the parents. Kids, particularly in stepfamilies, should be protected from exposure to adults' sexual activity, and a closed-door bedroom policy is the simplest and most effective way to provide that protection.

2. Allowing everyone, including children old enough to manage on their own, to have privacy for bathing or undressing. This is vital if the blended family includes opposite-sex teenagers, but it is important in any family.

3. Allowing kids to have privacy and space for doing homework, working on projects, or simply being by themselves.

4. Giving everyone some space that's completely their own. Even if children share bedrooms or only visit on weekends, each one should have at least a shelf, a box, or a dresser drawer that's private and safe from intrusion.

5. Allowing kids to have some toys or other special possessions that they don't have to share. Just because stepsisters or stepbrothers are the same age or share a bedroom doesn't automatically mean everything in the room is joint property.

6. No hitting, invasive tickling, or in other ways touching people when they don't want to be touched. Even a hug can be a violation if it is done to someone instead of being willingly shared.

7. No reading children's diaries, opening their mail, listening in on their telephone conversations, or searching their rooms. (There might be exceptions to this if you have reason to believe a child is in some kind of trouble such as stealing or using drugs—but it should never be done without serious justification.)

8. Not giving away or throwing out children's belongings without their knowledge. This is especially important if you are the stepparent and might not know the sentimental value of a child's possessions. If it's time to clean out the closet and get rid of outgrown clothes, let the kids help or do it all themselves if they're old enough.

9. Learning to accept that there are parts of your kids' lives that are none of your business, just as parts of your life are none of theirs. When children are young, our job as parents is to protect and teach them; we need to have a great deal of control over their lives. As they get older, however, our job changes. We need to move gradually out of the picture as they mature, letting them have increasing freedom to lead their own lives and have their own interests, opinions, and friends.

It's important that everyone in the family have permission to set boundaries about things that might matter to them, even if those same limits aren't important to someone else. Maybe two sisters are used to casually borrowing one another's clothes. That's fine as long as they're both comfortable. That doesn't mean their new stepsister should be expected to share her clothes in the same way if she doesn't want to.

It's also important that boundaries go two ways. At our house, Stephanie used to get furious if anyone borrowed her stuff or even went into her room without permission. But she would barge into the younger kids' rooms without knocking and help herself to their belongings. After some furious squawking from them and countless reminders from me, she finally learned to be a bit more respectful.

Learning to honor boundaries is important for easing the way within a blended family. It also can matter a great deal out in the "real world." Kids who haven't learned about limits are likely to interrupt, burst into other's rooms without knocking, casually use others' belongings without permission, invade others' personal space with inappropriate touching, and ask personal questions about matters that are none of their business. All of these behaviors will make them a serious pain in the neck. So you're acting in the long-term best interest of your kids and stepkids as well as the immediate comfort of your stepfamily when you insist on respect for one another's boundaries.

Courtesy and Respect

If I have guests in my house, particularly someone I like and respect, it's amazing what a patient and wise parent I can be. I find it much easier to use all of my best parenting skills when someone is watching. As a result, I have developed the ultimate guideline for good parenting and stepparenting:

If in doubt, treat your kids and stepkids the way you would if you had company.

I know, it sounds silly. But think about it for a minute. What tone of voice would you use with the kids if Mother Teresa were sitting in your living room? Or your best friend from college? Or your favorite teacher? How patient and reasonable could you be if you knew your boss or your minister were listening? Would you say "please" and "thank you" more often if the President were at your dinner table?

Or consider what would happen if you treated the kids in your household the way you would if they were guests. This doesn't mean that you should act with exaggerated formality, wait on them, and pick up after them, but that you extend the same courtesy you would most likely show to their friends.

If you had a foreign exchange student living with you, would you scream at her for not cleaning her room or would you politely insist that she finish it? Would you react differently if your friend's child or your own spilled milk at the table? If a visiting relative backed your car over the begonias, how would you respond to their apology? What if your daughter or your stepson did the same thing?

It's true that families ought to be places where we are free to be ourselves. But while we're doing that, we might as well be our best selves instead of our worst. Don't keep courtesy and respect stored in the closet like the fine china, to be brought out only on special occasions. Use them every day, for the people you care about the most. "Company manners" are really too important to keep just for guests. Family members deserve them, too.

Courtesy is also a valuable tool for building bridges with your stepkids. As you're working to bond with kids who are at least tentatively willing to let you into their lives, basic kindness and good manners will ease the way for all of you. It's tougher to be courteous, of course, if you're faced with resentful stepkids who don't treat you with even basic politeness. Do it anyway, as best you can. Make the effort to say a pleasant "good morning" day after day, even if you don't get an answer. Be the first to say "please" and "thank you" and "excuse me." It's likely to help you feel better about the effort you're making, it demonstrates that you're not letting them "get" you with their rudeness, and it keeps you from sinking to a childish "nyah, nyah" level of conflict.

Politeness only goes so far, though. It's probably the wisest policy, especially in the beginning, to overlook or rise above some rude remarks, snide comments meant for you to "accidentally" overhear, and minor challenges to your authority. However, you don't have to tolerate being disobeyed, being called names or sworn at, having your possessions taken or misused, or other types of abuse or disrespect. If you have any of this kind of conflict in your household, it's crucial that you and your spouse work together to deal with it. Most of the time kids who are faced with a united front and consistent consequences for rudeness or misbehavior will change. If they don't, you might need some tougher intervention or professional help.

If you've been polite, been pleasant, given kids plenty of time and space to get used to the new stepfamily, and they are still treating you like last year's dirty socks, eventually it may be time to get mad. If you think you need to do this, don't just let your frustration spill over some night at the supper table and start screaming. Instead, do your best to get angry like an adult. Don't whine or blame or start shoveling out guilt. Just let the family know clearly, congruently, and strongly that you have had enough and that you are putting your foot down. It's essential here that you have your spouse's support. (If you don't have it, maybe your spouse is the first person you need to confront.) Only the two of you can judge in your particular situation whether it's time to draw the line. If you do decide the time has come, your anger will have a lot more validity and authority behind it if you have treated your stepkids with courtesy and respect up to that point.

Kids aren't the only people who are entitled to good manners and respect from you. It's your job to use them with former spouses, too, even if they don't reciprocate. One component of that is just plain old courtesy—politeness in phone conversations about scheduling or visitation, letting non-custodial parents know about school events or achievements, having kids ready on time and with appropriate clothes if they are being picked up. Another component is respecting living arrangements at kids' other households.

Some examples of how *not* to do this:

A few years ago, when Dean's kids moved in for their six months with us, Peter brought a friend with him—an eight-inch black salamander with green speckles. I really didn't have anything against Sal, as long as nobody insisted that I let him crawl up my arm with his scratchy little feet. And I suppose being expected to go to the pet store once a week and buy crickets for his lunches wasn't especially unreasonable. But my real objection was that nobody asked my opinion about him before he moved in. Peter traded a turtle for him that summer at his mother's house, and when the kids came back here, it was just assumed Sal would come along. Dean and I would have appreciated being consulted first instead of being presented with a salamander fait accompli.

A friend of mine was faced with a similar situation, minus the crickets. Her young daughter, who had to share a room with her stepsister, complained to her father about feeling crowded at her mother's house. Trying to be helpful, he bought her a desk and a large toy chest to keep her private things in. Trouble was, there was absolutely no space in the girls' shared room to put two new pieces of furniture. His intervention, done without getting the

71

mother's opinion, just made the situation worse. It created more resentment between the girls and made the mother angry at his seeming interference. This was only settled by the daughter taking the desk and box back to her dad's house, where she used them on visits.

This same father, after learning that his teenage son would not be allowed to have his own phone line at his mother's house, bought him a telephone for his birthday. Again, the gift just created resentment.

Dean's sister, moving to another state, presented 12-year-old Stephanie with her old television set. Stephanie was thrilled. Her mother, who didn't care whether she had a TV in her room, thought it was fine. Dean and I, who don't think the kids should have their own TV's, wound up being the heavies who said, "No, you can't bring the TV to our house." We wouldn't have been placed in that position if his sister had thought to ask us before she offered her gift.

By now the point ought to be obvious. If your kids or stepkids live in two households, don't provide them with pets, furniture, or other large objects that affect the other household without checking first.

Unless you have serious reason to believe that a child is being abused or treated unfairly, living arrangements and rules at the other house are none of your business. Children may have to share rooms or may not be allowed privileges you think they should have. They will probably tell you all about these abuses in plaintive tones. But before you leap in there to do something about it, make sure your intervention won't just cause more problems. Do your part to ease tensions by treating the parents in the other household with the same consideration you would hope to receive from them.

Six

I Don't Like You and I Never Will!
The Myth of Instant Love

"You're Going to Just Love Each Other"

Suppose for a minute that you are a woman who has been happily married for ten years. As far as you know, everything is just fine the way it is. How would you feel if your husband came home one day with another woman—someone you've both known for some time—and said, "Hi, honey, this is your new sister-wife. She's going to share our bedroom. I told her she could wear your new dress to work tomorrow. Oh, and by the way, please make a copy of your car keys because she'll need to use your car half the time. I'm sure you're going to love each other." Would you welcome this interloper with enthusiastic warmth? Fat chance.

So why should we expect our kids to welcome new stepbrothers and stepsisters? Even if they've known each other for a while, even if they like each other, the reality of living under the same roof is unsettling. Suppose I'm a kid who has managed to adjust to my parents' divorce and settle into the routine of a single-parent family. All of a sudden here is another kid or two or three needing Mom or Dad's attention, getting into my things, maybe sharing my room, maybe operating under different family rules. And I'm being told this is my sister or brother and I should love them.

Some stepbrothers and sisters may like each other from the start. Others may not. It's usually safer for parents to assume the latter. And that's not easy. As parents in a new relationship, we need to believe that our kids are happy along with us. We want them to like each other and like the stepfamily. After all, we put them into this situation. If they aren't happy in it, that could imply we didn't make the best choice. So it's easy to disregard their feelings and send them a message of "Of course you like it here. Shut up and be happy."

But kids in a blended family will be happier in the long run if we don't force them to pretend to be happy in the beginning. Their feelings need to be acknowledged. It is important for all the kids involved in a stepfamily to have permission, especially in the beginning, not to like one another. Depending on the family situation and the kids' ages, that permission may be implied. In some cases, it may be helpful to tell kids clearly and directly, "You don't have to like each other."

There is an important "yeah-but" here. Along with permission not to like each other, kids need clear and direct guidelines about behavior. A feeling isn't the same thing as an action. Yes, it's okay not to like your stepsister. No, it's not okay to call her "you stupid cow" or put banana peels in her bed or pinch her when you think no one is looking. It's your job as a parent and stepparent to insist on courtesy and at least surface respect.

Keep in mind, as well, that accepting your kids' feelings is not the same thing as letting them control the family. If your kids resent someone you are dating or are angry because you plan to remarry, that doesn't necessarily mean you are doing anything wrong. If there is serious conflict between your fiancé and your kids, that is an issue you all need to deal with. If this person is abusive, treats your kids badly, or doesn't want to be involved with them, then you'd better take time for some second thoughts and maybe some professional advice about the relationship. If stepsiblings are beating each other up, destroying one another's belongings, or running away from home, it's time for some serious intervention such as family counseling.

But normal resentments, jealousies, and fears are not grounds for letting your kids dictate your relationships. One stepfamily book gave an example of a couple who postponed their marriage for 10 years—until the wife's daughters were both out of college—because the daughters didn't want their life disrupted. That is ridiculous. If one of those daughters had fallen in love and wanted to marry, do you suppose she would have postponed the wedding for years out of consideration for her mother?

So acknowledge your kids' fears and feelings, but maintain your bottom line. It's important to let kids know clearly that the basic situation won't change because of their differences. "I know it's hard for you, but we married because we love each other and all of us are living together and that's the way it is." Give the kids a set of boundaries to work with so they know just where they stand. This lets them know they don't have the power to manipulate parents and stepparents into changing the situation. It pushes them to direct their energy toward getting along in the stepfamily, rather than trying to destroy it.

Choosing to Love

When you first become a stepparent, you are faced with a fundamental choice. You can decide not to love your stepchildren, or you can decide to love them. This basic choice is tremendously important, because it will affect all the other choices you make as you interact with the other members of your stepfamily.

You need to make this decision once as the foundation for your relationship with your stepkids. But you aren't finished then. Once you've made the basic choice, you follow it up with a series of smaller day-to-day choices. You get to decide over and over whether to be loving or resentful.

Choosing not to love your stepchildren sometimes seems as if it would be the easier choice. If you just stay out of their lives and try to keep them out of yours, you can avoid all that messy stuff like pain and conflict. This may be an attractive theory—but the trouble is, it doesn't work that way. If you decide not to love your stepkids, you are paving the way for jealousy, resentment, and heartache on both sides.

So you might as well accept the fact that choosing to love your stepchildren is the best way to go. Love is the only tool strong enough to hold up under the challenges of living in a blended family.

All of that sounds very cosmic and grandiose. It ought to be accompanied by violin music or a New Age pan flute—or at least someone playing, "What The World Needs Now Is Love, Sweet Love," on the kazoo.

But before we all get carried away on a fluffy pink cloud of sentiment, let me clarify just what I mean by being loving. First of all, choosing to love your stepchildren doesn't necessarily have anything to do with feeling loving toward them. How you *feel* about them isn't the point. How you *act* toward them is.

One of my favorite definitions of love is one by Dr. M. Scott Peck in his book, *The Road Less Traveled*: "The will to extend one's self for the purpose of nurturing one's own or another's spiritual growth."

You notice that there's nothing in this definition about feelings. You don't have to feel loving toward someone in order to extend yourself on their behalf. You don't even have to like them—which is one of the things I appreciate about Dr. Peck's definition. When you become part of a blended family, you might find yourself living with people that you didn't necessarily choose and you don't necessarily like. It's comforting to know it's possible to treat those people with love even if you don't like them.

Love, the way Dr. Peck defines it, is an active choice which takes effort and courage. But ironically, if you are willing to expend that effort, you will find that choosing to be loving is a practical, day-to-day way of behaving that makes life easier. It's changing your actions in small ways that help you live more comfortably with the other members of your family.

76

Remember, we're not talking about saving the planet here. We're talking about choosing to say a pleasant, "Good morning" every day to a surly teenager who may ignore you. Or choosing to confront an issue that bothers you instead of pretending it isn't there. Or making the effort to get to know your stepkids instead of ignoring them. We're talking about plain old trying to get along better.

What we're not talking about is becoming a doormat. Some years ago I read a quotation by Emmet Fox which started out, "There is no difficulty that enough love will not conquer." I took his statement to mean that if I were only nice enough, if I only gritted my teeth and kept smiling, and if I overlooked anything negative, everything would be fine. It didn't work. Instead, I got squashed. If you let someone abuse you or another member of the family because you are too afraid to speak up, you are acting out of cowardice instead of love. You are nurturing neither your own spiritual growth nor that of the person who is being abusive.

When one person in a blended family chooses to act with Dr. Peck's kind of effortful love, there is a ripple effect. It may not be huge, and it may take time, but changes for the better will happen.

It's unlikely, however, that one of those changes will be growing to love your stepchildren exactly the way you love your children. As parents, we have bonds with our children that were first created with their conception. Threads were added to those bonds each time we held them, tucked them into bed, played with them, taught them, worried over them, rejoiced over them, fought with them. We see in their features and characteristics our own and those of our parents. They are the continuation of our bloodline, the passing down of our heritage. Even during times of conflict, even if we are sometimes indifferent or uncaring as parents, those bonds remain.

When stepchildren come into our lives, of course we don't have the same bonds. How could we? We weren't there when they were born, when they learned to walk, when they spent time in the hospital with pneumonia. We don't know them in the same way we know our own children. And they don't know us. Bonds need to be created between us slowly, over time, as we live together and learn about each other and fight and share.

Even after years as a stepfamily, even after genuine love has grown between you, the bonds with your stepchildren probably aren't going to be the same as the ones you have with your children. This is normal. Don't worry about it. What matters is that you treat all the kids in your stepfamily with respect, fairness, and as much love as you can. What matters is that you do create bonds with your stepchildren, bonds which can grow to be extremely close and can enrich all of your lives.

Choosing to Like

Do you like your stepkids? "Of course I love them," you say. "I knew they were part of the package when we got married, and I love them because I love their mother." I know that, but do you *like* them?

Almost every book or article I've ever read about parenting talks about how important it is for kids to feel loved. I think it's just as important for them to feel liked. Just think for a minute about what we do out of love and what we do out of liking. I take my kids and stepkids to the dentist, feed them nutritious foods, make them do chores, and discipline them because I love them. Those things are important, and I'm certainly not discounting them. But I could do all of them from a position of power, with a sense of martyrdom or annoyance, grimly out of a sense of duty, or absently without paying much attention to each child's individuality—and that might still be called love.

Liking, though is different. Liking is laughing at a kid's jokes, delighting in his talents, telling the rest of the family at the supper table about something clever he did or said, sharing his indignation at a friend's unkindness, and in general enjoying his company.

Love may be the foundation on which a blended family is built, but liking is the atmosphere that makes it worthwhile to live there.

So while you are choosing to love your stepkids and nurture their spiritual growth, see if you can make your life and theirs more pleasant by learning to like them as well. Depending on your family situation, this may be really tough. It's easy to like a three-year-old who is cute, funny, and happy to have you as part of the family. It's not so easy to like a twelve-year-old who is rude, resentful, and attempting to get rid of you.

Dealing with a stepchild who doesn't want you around can generate incredibly petty impulses, jealousies, and dislikes in your innermost soul, even if you are normally a reasonably sane and mature adult. Indulge in private fantasies of revenge if you have to, whine or vent your frustrations once in a while with a friend or a support group—but don't act on those impulses at home. This is an "act as if" situation. Treat your stepkids as if you liked them. (This may mean something as basic as resisting the impulse to turn on the hot water in the kitchen while your annoying stepson is in the shower.)

Dealing with the challenge of trying to like someone who doesn't like you might be a bit easier if you remember these ideas:

1. Keep in mind that the part of this stepchild which doesn't like you is a fearful little kid, even if this is a teenager who is six foot two in his socks. The basis for their resentment and dislike is fear of losing something—most likely their relationship with their parent. Do your best to deal with that little kid on the inside, not the powerful-appearing person on the outside.

2. There has to be something likable about this kid—who, after all, is your spouse's child. You certainly wouldn't have married someone who parented a monster, would you?

3. Keep your ego out of the way as much as you can. It isn't necessarily you personally who is disliked, it is the stepparent role that you have.

4. If you have any common interests at all, build on them. Maybe you both like computers or shopping or the Sunday night

movie. It's especially helpful if there is something you can have your stepchild teach you—it can be a way to spend pleasant time together, and it's a constructive way to satisfy their need to be powerful.

5. Use the power of touch. This doesn't mean you should start grabbing astonished teenagers for hugs neither of you is ready for. But consciously begin touching your stepkids in small friendly ways—perhaps a hand on their shoulder as you're helping with homework or a touch on the arm as you give them lunch money or the car keys. If the relationship is difficult, particularly with older kids, start slowly and neutrally with almost unnoticeable touches. You don't want to be invasive here, but take advantage of any opportunity you have to send friendly non-verbal messages through touch.

6. Praise is a powerful agent of change. Finding something about a difficult stepchild to sincerely praise can be a tiny beginning to a better relationship. The key word here is "sincere." Don't try to build liking by suddenly gushing over with empty compliments. Find something you genuinely approve of, no matter how small. Maybe the surly teenager who hates being part of a stepfamily and wears dirty grunge clothes and whose room is a hazardous waste area takes great care of his car. Or gets to school on time every day. Or has great hair. Once you dig out that first something, others are easier to find. But these compliments need to be given with no strings attached—no expectation of a change in the kids' behavior or an immediate lessening of tension. Because this kind of praise isn't to change the other person, it's to change the way you perceive them. If you can't find anything to praise about someone, you are seeing them as one-dimensional and not good enough to relate to. When you begin to see even a little thing about them which deserves praise, you start to accept the possibility that they are someone you might be able to like and respect.

From "His Bratty Kid" to "My Sister" Takes Time

If you are just starting out as a stepfamily and are despairing of these kids ever learning to get along, remember that relationships within the family will evolve over time. Take two examples from our stepfamily:

A. Rachel and Amy are nearly the same age and are in the same grade in school. They have quite different personalities, interests, and priorities. Their feelings toward one another have gone through a series of changes over the years. In the beginning, as first graders, they were excited about having a same-age sister. They wanted bunk beds in their shared room, borrowed one another's clothes, and were going to be best friends. That lasted for a while. But sharing a bedroom got to be a pain in the neck for both of them, what with Amy's talking in her sleep and Rachel's untidiness, and for a few years they had periods of shaky friendship alternating with active dislike. Being able to move into separate bedrooms when they were eleven helped a lot.

Now, as young teenagers, they have different sets of friends, different priorities in their lives, and different interests. If they knew each other from school they probably wouldn't be more than casual friends. They still annoy each other sometimes because of their differences. But I often hear them talking in one or the other's bedroom at night. They borrow clothes and share nail polish, ask each other's advice about what to wear, and back each other up whenever one of them is mad at me. In other words, they act like most sisters. They don't necessarily like each other all the time, but they do like each other quite a bit of the time, and in general they co-exist comfortably.

B. Loren and Stephanie, 13 and 10 respectively when we first started out as a stepfamily, had a lot of overt conflict in the beginning. Stephanie challenged Loren for the "oldest kid" position. They teased and goaded each other. He thought she was stupid and bossy; she thought he was stupid and a slob. It wasn't a lot of fun. As they got used to each other and to the family situation, the conflict receded. They started to play board games together, join forces once in a while against the younger kids, and form a tentative alliance. This lasted through two six-month cycles when all the kids were living with us.

The third winter, Loren went to live with his dad, so he and Stephanie didn't ever really have a chance to get comfortable together. Now, as young adults, the two of them visit pleasantly at family get-togethers but don't really interact otherwise. They don't actively dislike or fight with one another; they just don't have much in common or care very much about each other. Their lives are going in different directions, and there really isn't much point in pushing them to get together or develop a relationship.

It's important to accept the reality that it will take time—lots of time—for kids to learn to like each other. That doesn't mean your job as a parent and stepparent is to bury your head in your pillow and wait until they decide to be civil. Part of your job is to create a situation to make it easier for them to become friends. So let's get down to some nuts and bolts of helping kids learn to like each other:

1. Having their own space matters a whole lot. I believe Amy and Rachel would have gotten along much more comfortably if they had not had to share a bedroom for the first five years. Family resources and budgets are limited, and it simply isn't always possible for kids to have rooms of their own. But everybody needs someplace that is their own space, safe from intrusion—even if that is only a dresser drawer or a toy chest. And I would strongly recommend that you scrimp in other areas, such as vacations or newer cars, if as a result you can move to a house big enough for family members to stay out of one another's space.

2. It can be helpful if the blended family starts out in a house that is neutral territory, rather than one which was someone's

previous home. It's easier to share a room with a new stepsibling if that room isn't the same one you've had all to yourself for six or seven years. It's easier to accept a stepdad sharing a bedroom with Mom if it isn't the same bedroom your dad used to sleep in. It's easier to start out in a house that's new to everyone, rather than have some family members feeling as if their territory is being invaded and other members feeling like intruders.

3. Set an example of courtesy, and expect everybody to follow it. Make it clear that you will not tolerate behavior such as name-calling, hitting, and taking or destroying someone else's belongings.

4. Be fair. Rules and privileges for kids need to be evenhanded. Maybe your nine-year-old has been allowed to roam the neighborhood freely, while your spouse's ten-year-old has been required to account for his whereabouts at all times. The new family needs to have a new rule, maybe somewhere in the middle, that applies to both of them. Amounts of allowances, curfews, use of cars, and all the other countless parenting decisions need to be worked out between the parents as equitably as possible.

5. Don't push too fast. You don't have to insist that your daughter introduce your husband's daughter as "my sister"—though you may want to have a private conversation if you hear descriptions such as "stepnerd." Don't demand that younger kids share all their toys or older kids loan their clothes or other belongings.

6. Manage the household to reduce friction. This means dealing with the small causes that can have such big effects. Maybe your 14-year-old daughter loves to take long showers and fuss over her hair in the bathroom every morning. That was fine when the household was just the two of you. It will cause huge amounts of conflict if she continues it with three stepsiblings waiting in line at the door. It's your job as a parent to limit her time in the bathroom to be fair to others in the family, while providing alternatives like a good makeup mirror in her bedroom so she can still feel gorgeous when she heads out the door.

7. Emphasize the kids' differences in a positive way. It's unreasonable to expect your stepdaughter to go out for band just because your two daughters do, or to think your stepson should care about football because your son does. Maybe one kid is a track star who gets average grades. Maybe another is an honor roll student. Maybe one is a slob but has a great sense of humor. Applaud and praise all their achievements, not just the ones that you are used to thinking of as important.

8. Never, ever, ever compare kids to each other. If you ever hear yourself saying, "Why can't you get A's like Jenny?" or "Andy always manages to keep his room clean," take yourself straight to the bathroom, wash your mouth out with soap, and then go write fifty times, "I will not compare." Kids will compare themselves with each other and will compete with each other on their own—don't you dare do it to them. You will create resentments which will come back to haunt you.

9. Don't overdo listening to your kids' resentments. Your children are likely to come to you with horrible tales of the indignities they suffer at the hands of their stepbrothers or stepsisters. They will omit to mention any provocation on their part. Let them express their feelings, deal with problems and conflicts as fairly as you can, but don't overdo the sympathy. Remember that your own little darlings are neither perfect nor blameless. If you pair with them and encourage them to feel abused, you will make it harder for everyone to work out the conflict in a constructive way.

10. Don't gossip with your kids about your stepkids. It is quite likely that you will share some of your children's irritation about annoying habits your stepchildren have. Maybe you have taught your kids always to ask permission before they borrow things, while your stepkids have been brought up to be more casual about using other people's stuff. You and your kids are both likely to find this irritating. Deal with the problem, by all means. But don't foster an "us vs. them" atmosphere by talking with your kids about it behind your stepkids' backs.

11. Don't force kids to share their friends. If your seven-year-old son is invited to a birthday party, that doesn't mean your eight-year-old stepson has to be invited as well. If your twelve-year-old stepdaughter has a friend spend the night, they shouldn't have to automatically include your ten-year-old daughter in their late-night giggling. (Neither, by the way, should it be okay for them to be actively rude to her. Maybe she could have one of her friends sleep over, as well—or better yet, spend the night at a friend's house.)

12. Remember that everyone in the blended family has the right and responsibility to develop their own relationships with the other family members. You may wish desperately that your son and your stepdaughter would like each other. Maybe they never will. You can insist that they be courteous, you can treat them both as fairly as you can, but you cannot make them love each other.

13. Decide as a couple just what participation in family activities you expect from the kids. If you go on a family outing, does everybody have to come along or can they choose to stay home or do something with their friends instead? Is everyone expected to show up at the family dinner table, or can they make themselves a peanut butter sandwich on their way out the door or park themselves and their plates in front of the TV set? The level of participation isn't what matters so much here (though I am strongly prejudiced in favor of more rather than less). The important thing is that different expectations should be based on kids' ages rather than whose kids they are.

14. Do stuff together. I know, this somewhat contradicts number 13. But you simply can't grow to like someone until you get to know them. And you get to know them by spending time with them. Conversations around the dinner table, family hikes or fishing trips, going out for ice cream, working in the yard together—all of these are family-builders.

It works best if these expeditions and projects are voluntary, with the kids invited to come along rather than being told they have to come. But especially with younger kids, a little coercion isn't all bad. I don't know how many times, when Peter was smaller, that I took him with me to get groceries or run an errand when he didn't want to go. We would start out with him moaning and complaining—how come he always had to go along, and how come I didn't think he was old enough to stay home by himself, and how stupid this was, and how his mother never made him go somewhere if he didn't want to. This would last for a few blocks or a few minutes. Then he would notice something outside the car or remember something that happened at school, forget how much he was being abused, and start talking. We would chat for the rest of the trip and have a perfectly comfortable time.

If your family-building time is a chore such as raking leaves or cleaning the garage, then there's nothing whatsoever wrong with making it required for everybody. The bonding still happens, especially if the adults in the party tackle the project with cheerfulness and enthusiasm. (If nothing else, the kids might all join together in united resentment against the parents—and a little bit of that kind of bonding can be useful, too.)

15.   Give family-building its proper priority. One of the best things that happened to us in the early days of our stepfamilying was my getting laid off from a challenging and demanding job. I couldn't find another one right away, so I began a part-time business which I managed from home. Because of that change, I was much more available to all the kids than I would have been otherwise. My being able to give parenting and stepparenting a major share of my time and energy for that first year was a life-saver for us. We could have used the money I had been earning, but at that point in our lives my attention and presence at home was needed far more. When you are just beginning a stepfamily, that's not the time to take on heavy demands at work or in community activities. Devote all the energy you possibly can to the family in those early years. It might involve some financial or career compromises, but it's an investment you absolutely won't regret.

Don't Know Much About History

Once when Peter was four, he came down with a bad cold, and I decided some cough medicine was in order. I dug out the bottle and a spoon, got ready to pour, and said, "Come take some of this; it will help your cough."

I expected him to open wide. Instead, he headed the other direction in a hurry.

I was completely taken aback for a minute. My experience with my two kids was that taking medicine was no big deal. Neither of them had been sick very much, and most children's medicine came in cherry or bubble-gum flavors, so we'd never had any conflict about taking it.

But I had forgotten that Peter's history was different. He was born with a twisted foot and had major surgery when he was just a year old. He had seen so many doctors and swallowed so much bad-tasting medicine that he was anything but matter-of-fact about taking the stuff.

Once I remembered why Peter wasn't likely to be enthusiastic about taking cough syrup, it was easy to be patient. I spent a few minutes explaining why the medicine would help his cough, tasted it myself and told him honestly what it tasted like, got him a glass of water to wash it down, and praised him when he wrinkled up his nose and gulped.

Peter is twelve now and has long since become nonchalant about taking medicine. But what if I hadn't known his history that day when he was four? What if I had assumed he was just being contrary or stubborn and hadn't taken the time to be patient with him? I'm not saying I'd have ruined Peter's life by having a big fight with him about cough medicine. But at that point, when we were just getting to know each other, the conflict certainly wouldn't have done our relationship any good. Because I knew that particular piece of Peter's history, I was able to use the medicine-taking to build a bridge between us. If I hadn't known it, building the bridge would have been more difficult.

Every interaction we have with another person is colored by what we know of that person's history. In general, the more we know about them, the more understanding and compassion we will have as we relate to them. So learning as much history as possible about our stepchildren is important.

Sometimes those missing pieces of history result in awkward situations. Most stepparents are familiar with those "routine" questions that stump us at unexpected times. "Has she had all her immunizations?" "Name and address of the child's physician." "We'll need his social security number." These may be uncomfortable or embarrassing, but they're minor and often funny. The real importance of learning family history goes far beyond dates and vaccinations.

Is Jeremy afraid of enclosed spaces because his sister locked him in the closet and forgot about him when he was two? Does Maggie have a special bond with her grandmother because Grandma babysat for her when she was little? Is Angie's constant challenging of her stepmother's authority because Angie has always been in charge of the younger kids? Does Tony feel like the dumb one in the family because school is harder for him than for his older brother?

This is the kind of history that matters the most in building a blended family. Taking the time to learn it is well worth the effort. It's another way of letting the kids know you care about them. It builds understanding and compassion. And it helps mesh their history with yours, so you become more fully a family.

"I Hate Him and I Hate You and I Wish You Didn't Live Here!"

It saves wear and tear if you accept the fact that there is going to be conflict and anger in your stepfamily. Sometimes tension can simmer beneath the surface for a long time, or sometimes it can erupt in open conflict. We were lucky at our house—it blew up quickly into outright civil war. Hostilities broke out two weeks after we had all started living together for the first time, just as Dean and I were congratulating ourselves on how well everything seemed to be working out. We had both gone to a meeting, leaving the five kids home. We came back three hours later to a household in uproar, with Loren shut up in his room, the three little ones wild-eyed and excited instead of in bed where they belonged, and Stephanie offering a shamefaced confession: "The holes in his door are where I hit it with the baseball bat."

We never did quite figure out exactly how it started or get the exact sequence of events. We did piece together from the conflicting stories that there was some disagreement over which of the older two was in charge of getting the younger ones to bed. They starting exchanging insults, the other three chose up sides and joined in, and the battle was on. It was a bit like World War I— nobody was sure what the original dispute was about, but they had family commitments to honor so they plunged in anyway. There was a lot of screaming, Loren started making threats with a broken BB gun, Stephanie locked him out of the house, the little kids went on the offensive by throwing things down the basement steps, Loren got back in and strategically withdrew to his room, Stephanie attacked his door with the baseball bat—and an hysterical time was had by all. Stephanie finally called her mother, who came over and imposed a truce until we got home. At least the door was the only casualty.

Even now, looking back after eight years, this is still more embarrassing than anything else. I hope that someday it will be funny. For me it was an added humiliation to have my stepkids' mother involved. I hated having Jeri know first-hand that we weren't running a perfect household, and I was afraid she would decide she didn't want to share custody if her kids were going to be living in such chaos. (At that point I still operated in the fantasy that there wasn't any conflict in her new blended family.)

But one thing you can say for the great civil war—it certainly did get our attention. Its short-term result was that Dean and I imposed some consequences and established clearer ground rules. The kids apologized, paid for the damage to the door and had to get along for a while without the baseball bat and the BB gun. We set some specific rules about the kind of behavior we expected and who was in charge when we were gone. The long-term result was more important. The outbreak of hostilities forced us to give up our fantasy of having the perfect blended family without having to work at it.

By now, even though I'm still embarrassed about it, I can be grateful for this incident. It was dramatic enough to force us to pay attention to the conflicts among the kids, and it happened early enough in our stepfamilying that the tension hadn't solidified into lasting resentments. It would have been easy to close our eyes to the conflict the kids were feeling and build a myth of perfectly happy children in the perfect blended family. Fortunately, the kids didn't let us do that.

Not all blended families are lucky enough to have conflicts brought into the open in such an unignorable fashion. One not-quite-blended-yet family I know includes two teenage stepsisters who have never been given a chance to deal openly with their anger about the changed family situation. The girls hate each other's guts. They go their separate ways at school except for the verbal digs they toss at each other whenever they have a chance. They take out their anger on each other with malicious sly pinches, "humorous" put-downs and "accidents" that mess up the other's clothes or room. Yet in front of their parents both of them are carefully polite through gritted teeth. They don't dare be anything else and destroy the adults' fantasies about how well everyone gets along. They don't even argue the way they would if they had been raised together. (Which absence of conflict ought to be the first clue that something is wrong.) The parents, clinging firmly to the image of their successful blended family, think everything is fine.

Keeping up the fiction of happy children who always get along is much easier than dealing with the fact of real kids who are sometimes furious with their parents and stepparents for disrupting their lives. We want our new blended family to be happy for everyone, and sometimes we just can't quite see the ways that it doesn't meet that ideal.

In a stepfamily that has set up an image that "we're doing this perfectly," kids don't dare talk about their fear or their anger. But sooner or later that buried anger and frustration is likely to explode in some other direction. Any child in a blended family who claims everything is fine but who starts getting into trouble at school, shoplifting, having frequent illnesses or acting out some other way is probably signaling that there are issues to be worked out at home.

I used to hate it when Stephanie would tell me bitterly, "Loren never does anything right and you don't even care—you always let him get by with it just because he's your son. And you never let me get by with anything." It was just as difficult when Loren would fume at me, "Stephanie bugs me and bugs me and you don't ever do anything about it—if you don't make her behave I'm going to beat her up." At times like this it was hard to remember the evenings when the two of them would play Monopoly or Nintendo in perfect amity. I hated trying to work out the conflicts between them, especially when the only result seemed to be to make both of them mad at me. (I finally figured out that if both of them were accusing me of being unfair, it was a sign that I was probably doing something right.)

It's hard to accept the fact that the kids sometimes hate us, each other or the family situation we chose for them. Letting that conflict out into the open so it can be faced is a challenge. It's tempting to bury it instead with reactions like, "of course you like each other," or, "you all need to get along and I don't want to hear any more of this nonsense." What we need to do instead is listen to kids' feelings, keep the rules as clear and reasonable as possible, and address specific problems as fairly as we can.

It also helps to keep clearly in mind that these kids would fight if they had all been born into the same family. Any time you have more than one child in a household, there will be conflicts over who gets to watch which television channel, who has to put the corn flakes away, who fed the cat last, and who left the mess in the bathroom. Each one's room is sacred ground to be defended from all potential invaders. They all view their own stuff with holy regard—which doesn't mean they will keep it put away or that they will extend the same courtesy to the property of others. And they all have their fairness antennae out at all times to be sure somebody else isn't getting by with something. Having a blended family just adds another dimension to those conflicts. It isn't necessarily the cause of all of them.

All those conflicts don't get resolved by pretending they don't exist. The kids won't get along peacefully just because I want them to. They'll get along peacefully by working out their problems. And that working-out process isn't always nice. I find it helpful to remind myself that anger sometimes is just a tool to bring a problem out into the open so it can be solved.

I used to think every parent should be issued a referee's shirt when their second child joined the family. As I learn more about what is my business and what isn't, I've decided to turn my striped shirt and whistle back in. I'm resigning. Now, when a child comes to me with tears of righteous indignation welling in her eyes to tell me, "She's being so mean and it isn't fair," I can often respond with, "Then you need to go work that out with her." If two kids come to me to mediate a dispute, the most appropriate response often is, "You two negotiate and figure it out."

This teaches kids that the first one who tattles isn't necessarily right. More important, it lets them know they have the power to work out differences and find a solution. Much of the time they are able to do exactly that. Of course, there are still some times when it's a parent's job to intervene. Little kids need our help to solve problems; we need to teach them about sharing and taking turns and leaving other people's stuff alone. Older kids need guidelines for constructive disagreements so their battles don't degenerate into ugly bouts of name-calling. At our house, I usually feel a need to step in when:

1. Someone starts hitting or calling names.

2. Older kids are bullying or taking advantage of younger ones.

3. The fight has gone on for a while, is escalating, and no resolution seems to be in sight.

4. The fight is over a long-standing issue that the kids haven't been able to resolve.

5. The noise gets to a level I can't stand.

Letting the kids learn to do their own fighting has been challenging for me. I still want to say, "Just stop it and be nice to each other!" But I know it's important to let them learn how to resolve conflicts. And I've also learned that this hands-off approach helps me treat kids and stepkids more fairly. Even after eight years, if my daughter and stepdaughter are fighting, my first gut reaction is to defend my daughter. Staying out of their smaller conflicts helps give me the perspective to be fair when I do need to step in.

By now, I'm slowly learning that now and then the first step toward solving a problem involves someone getting angry and maybe even some shouting. Sometimes the quickest way to end a conflict is to charge right straight through the middle. The process may not be pretty, but it gets the job done.

Add, Don't Subtract

The first time that my husband's kids came to live with us, I jumped headfirst into being SuperStepmom. I was sure I could be the best stepmother in the world—never mind the fact that I didn't necessarily know how to be the best mother in the world. I was going to love all the kids the same, treat them absolutely fairly, and have plenty of time and energy for everybody.

However, my Brady Bunch fantasies left out a few details. One of them was the reality of my own kids getting angry because they felt I was shoving them aside to make room for the three newcomers. I was so busy trying to bond with my stepkids that I forgot Loren and Rachel weren't necessarily interested in doing the same thing.

If you have children of your own and are working to build a new family which includes stepkids, remember that your kids still need you as much as they did before. Becoming a stepfamily means changes in the family structure, lifestyle, traditions, and patterns. But as you make those changes, do your best to keep the customs that are special to your kids. Continue established rituals such as reading bedtime stories. Make sure the hugs, kisses, and snuggling don't get lost in the chaos. Be patient with your kids as they get used to sharing you.

Remind yourself that love doesn't subtract or divide, it only adds and multiplies. Take the energy you need for stepfamilying away from your job, your community activities, your friends, or your hobbies, but never take it away from your own kids. They still need your reassurance that they are special, that they are loved, and that they won't be replaced in your life or your heart by your stepkids.

Seven

Taming the Terrible Trio—
Jealousy, Resentment, and Control

Jealousy

In a support group, Dave, a new stepfather, spoke up with some hesitation about his jealousy of his wife's two teenage sons. "I'm ashamed of feeling that way," he said. "I ought to be more mature than that."

Most new stepparents are somewhat prepared for stepchildren to be jealous of them. It can be a shock to recognize that the feeling goes both directions. But if you think about it, feeling jealous is a natural response for stepparents as well as stepkids.

As a traditional family develops, the parents first create their own bond as a couple. Then children come along, and the family evolves as they are born into it. In stepfamilies, the parents don't have that time to themselves first. Quite the contrary—the spouse's kids were there first. They have family history, traditions, and bonds that the new partner doesn't share. At a time when new couples want to focus on each other, there are others competing for time and attention, perhaps even actively trying to push the stepparent out of the family. Under these circumstances, jealousy is a normal feeling.

Like Dave, most stepparents are ashamed of feeling jealous of stepchildren. After all, you are an adult. You "shouldn't" feel that way. You "should" know better. But knowing better doesn't really have anything to do with it. The jealousy doesn't come from your mature adult self; it grows out of the part of you that is a little kid wanting to be loved and fearing someone else will take that love away.

Getting rid of this jealousy is important, because it can be enormously destructive in a stepfamily. There are several factors that help in dealing with it. Admitting to yourself that you feel jealous is an important first step. Acknowledging the feeling isn't the same as condoning it or allowing yourself to indulge in it. But you can't deal with jealousy if you're busy pretending you're not jealous.

Once you accept that it exists, you can use the jealousy as a messenger. In some cases the message might be simply, "This is normal; don't worry about it." If the feeling is occasional or intermittent, merely admitting its presence might be enough to help you cope with it.

Sometimes jealousy is a red flag that means something is wrong. This was true in Dave's situation. His new wife, needing to see herself as a good and committed mother, had her sons first on her list when it came to time and energy. Her job was second. Dave was trailing along in third, getting what was left over. In this case, his feeling of jealousy could be the first step for the two of them to address this problem. Unless she could change her priorities and invite Dave more fully into the family unit, their new stepfamily might not survive.

Most often, though, jealousy is sending a message that something is wrong on the inside, not the outside. If you feel jealous, it can be a signal that you need something—support, confidence, or reassurance that you are loved. The problem then becomes how to get what you need without taking it away from your stepkids, who need the same things.

You can and should get support outside the stepfamily, from friends, groups, or counseling. This is a place to share frustrations, learn skills, and build your confidence that you are doing okay as a person and a stepparent. You also need support from your spouse, because perhaps the most important factor in dealing with jealousy is feeling secure in your marriage. That security is built when you and your spouse back each other up in conflicts within the family, when you are there for each other consistently, and when you commit time and energy to each other. If you know that your spouse is committed to you, then you can feel safe enough to let your stepchildren get the attention they need without seeing it as a threat to you.

So if you are battling feelings of jealousy that are more than occasional flashes, it's important to share them with your spouse. Please do your best to talk about this in a way that simply admits the feelings and even acknowledges the irrationality of them. Don't use an approach of, "I'm jealous of your kids and you need to fix it by giving me more time and attention."

Showing your commitment to one another does mean sharing time and attention, of course. You and your spouse need to reserve some energy for each other. It's important that you work together to do so in a way that is constructive rather than destructive for your stepfamily.

There are some ways to help find some time to focus on each other without taking it away from the kids. If you both have children who live primarily with you but spend time at other parents' houses, do your best to make sure everybody is gone at the same time. Then you can do special family things together when all the kids are around to participate, and you and your spouse can have time alone when all of them are gone. Even an occasional kid-free weekend can be a valuable break. But time together doesn't have to come in large chunks. On a daily basis, take advantage of a few minutes here and there. Dean and I have some great conversations in the mornings while we're getting up, showering, and dressing. You can take walks in the evening while kids are doing homework or watching television—good for your physical as well as emotional health. Don't think that a date with each other necessarily has to be a major social occasion. Try getting together for lunch or going out for breakfast on Saturday mornings while the kids are sleeping in. Depending on your circumstances and the ages of your kids, there are bound to be times you can reserve for each other. Little kids go to bed early; older kids go out with friends and sleep late on weekends. Take advantage of those times—and don't use them all just to talk about Katie's grades or the problems with the plumbing, either. It's important to make good use of the time you do have together.

While it's important, time and attention for each other is only part of the answer to jealousy. Even more essential is a change in your attitude. Don't set this up as a competition, even if your stepkids have already done so. The only way you can "win" is to refuse to compete. Remember that you and the kids are not peers, contesting for the same kind of love from your spouse. Instead, see yourself and your spouse as partners, standing side by side as equals and working together to give the children in your family the love and attention they need.

When you see the relationships in this way, it becomes easier to invite stepchildren in rather than joining in a psychological sumo-wrestling contest to push one another out. Communicating and building closeness with your spouse helps the two of you feel secure within the circle of each other's love. Then you both can draw a larger circle which includes all the kids.

> *He drew a circle that shut me out,*
> *Heretic, rebel, a thing to flout.*
> *But Love and I had the wit to win.*
> *We drew a circle that took him in.*
> *Edwin Markham*

Resentment

Do you still remember—with vivid detail, brilliant color, and full surround sound—the first big fight you had with one of your stepkids? Do you still blush or stop breathing in sheer embarrassment when you recall mistakes you made several years ago? Are you still mad because your stepdaughter called you ugly names when she was eleven? Does your stomach hurt when you think about a conflict with your former spouse that happened a long time ago?

If you answer yes to your own version of these questions, then maybe you are holding on to stuff that you need to let go of. Maybe you've been keeping hurt and anger locked up until they turn into resentment.

Resentment is like the gunk that builds up on the sides of your bathtub. A little bit gets added with every bath, and you don't notice it much because it's such a small amount. Then all of a sudden one day you look at the tub, and there's a dingy gray ring all the way around it which is absolutely disgusting, and you know it's time to get out the cleaner and do something to get rid of it.

Resentment accumulates in the same way. Your favorite casserole is greeted with, "Eeewh, this is gross!" Your stepdaughter throws away one of your daughter's favorite books. Your stepson uses your car and doesn't live up to his agreement to fill the gas tank. Your mother calls, and none of your stepkids bother to give you the message. You tell your stepdaughter she needs to finish cleaning her room, and she calls you an ugly name under her breath. Each one of these is a wound to your ego, a jab at your feelings, or a setback to your attempts to bond with your stepkids. They aren't that huge individually, but a small layer of resentment gets added with each one, until one day you blow up and start screaming. The problem is complicated by the fact that each member of the family is likely to be collecting their own private set of resentments, and one blowup can trigger another.

Unfortunately, you can't get rid of accumulated resentment as easily as you can scrub away the crud in the bathtub. It is possible, though, to keep it from building up in the first place.

The answer to resentment is detachment. Detachment in a stepfamily has two important facets. One is choosing not to take things personally. The other is refusing to entangle yourself in what is not your business.

99

Not taking things personally is especially useful in protecting yourself from attacks by angry or resentful kids. If you take it personally every time there is a conflict, you'll go nuts in short order. Detachment can keep you from being hurt every time a four-year-old points out, "My real mom makes pancakes the right way," or an angry teenager shouts, "It makes me sick the way you two can't keep your hands off each other!" It helps you keep in mind that many times the resentments and frustrations of kids and stepkids have nothing to do with you as a person.

The idea of detachment is simple, but it's far from easy. You can't stop taking things personally just because you should. It helps to have some "how-to" suggestions. These are a few which have been helpful for me:

1. Try thinking of an angry child's behavior as a role, not as an inherent part of that person. In the play, *Our Stepfamily, Act Two,* it might be understandable for a child to be angry or resentful at a particular time. That means the anger is directed, not at you as a person, but at your role as a parent or stepparent. It would be there even if your role were being played by Michelle Pfeiffer or Tom Cruise. Then you have some choice over your own role in response. You can play the role of a victim, an angry and punishing wicked stepparent, or a compassionate and understanding adult.

2. Remember that just because an attack is sent doesn't mean it has to be accepted. The next time a child throws a zinger at you, try pretending that the words are inside a big beach ball. If someone tosses a beach ball at you, you have several choices: You can catch it and keep it, you can catch it and throw it back, you can let it bounce off you, or you can step aside out of its way. No matter what choice you make, you aren't going to get hurt by that light, harmless ball.

3. Try imagining that an angry message is being sent through the mail. What the child is saying is the letter. The anger they're sending along with it is the envelope. Mentally open the envelope, toss it in the trash, and then check out the letter. Maybe it says

something worth paying attention to; maybe it doesn't. It's easier to decide whether it's an important message or junk mail after you separate it from the anger surrounding it.

It's a challenge to stay detached and resist taking every criticism personally. It takes practice and work, helped along by a sense of humor. However, it's well worth the effort, both for your stepfamily's smoother functioning and your own peace of mind. Whatever strategies you try can do wonders for your serenity if you practice them. When you can keep your ego and your feelings out of the way, it's easier to deal calmly with the problem at hand. Then you can stay an adult as you remind your stepson to fill the gas tank, enforce some consequences for name-calling, or take the evaluation of your casserole as a culinary opinion rather than a personal insult.

Refusing to get involved in what isn't your business is the other part of detachment. Sometimes this means keeping your mouth shut when others don't do what you believe they should. Sometimes it means keeping yourself out of the middle of a conflict between two other members of your stepfamily.

The problem with being in the middle, of course, is that you get shot at from both sides. My friend Leann, who has been married and divorced three times and has two grown children from her first marriage, told me, "The part I absolutely hated was always being in the middle between my kids and my husband. I was always trying to keep everybody happy and make sure everything was okay. And I just couldn't do it."

To keep yourself out of the middle, remind yourself politely to "Mind your own business." First, of course, you need to pay attention to what is your business and what isn't. It is your business to see that kids and stepkids treat each other with a reasonable amount of respect. It isn't your business to make them like each other. Nor is it your business to make sure your spouse and your kids love each other. It isn't your job to keep everyone in the family happy. It is your business if former spouses don't pay child support that's due. It isn't your business whether the rules at their houses are the same as the ones at yours.

Sometimes, especially with smaller conflicts, it's relatively easy to decide that tension between two other family members isn't your business. Then you can just choose to step out of it and let them deal directly with each other. But minding your own business isn't the whole answer. When the conflict blew up in our family between Dean and Loren, I was in an awful position. I loved them both, and I was torn by painful feelings of divided loyalty. My frustration didn't come from meddling in what wasn't my business. It came from the pain of having two people I loved involved in a serious conflict that I couldn't fix.

In a situation like this, it isn't realistic to stop feeling caught in the middle. That's exactly where you are. What you can do, though, is choose not to behave like a puppet whose strings are being pulled from two directions. You don't have to take sides. It's okay to love both your spouse and your child. You don't have to agree with either of their judgments about each other, you can let them both know you don't like the situation, and you don't have to solve the problem.

When you stop acting like a frantically spinning top, trying to keep everyone else happy, you are choosing to have some respect for yourself and your middle ground. You may not be able to remove yourself completely from the middle, but you can reduce tension by treating that spot as neutral territory.

Neutrality, after all, is the underlying premise of detachment. When you detach from someone or some situation, you are staying out of the way and allowing other people to deal with the consequences of their own choices and their own actions. But remember that detachment is a friendly neutrality. The goal is detachment with love. It isn't withdrawing in bitterness or anger to "let someone get what's coming to them." It isn't hiding because your feelings are hurt or you don't think you can cope. It is making an active, loving choice to step aside and let others experience what they have the right and the need to experience. It is letting others in the family build their own relationships directly instead of seeing each other through your eyes.

Control

When you become part of a stepfamily, you will be given a valuable gift. You may not want it at first. You may even kick and scream and fight desperately not to take it. But if you do finally decide to accept it, you'll find that its value goes far beyond learning to live comfortably in a stepfamily. That gift is learning to let go.

The opposite of letting go, of course, is being in control. Most of us, deep in our selfish little hearts, would like to be in control all the time. We don't want anyone else to win. We don't want to be flexible. We don't want to share. We really would like to always get our own way. Of course, we won't always get it—a fact which we accept in varying degrees as we grow past the age of two. Maturity means learning to compromise, to adapt, and to become comfortable with the fact that sharing our lives with other people means giving up control over parts of it.

Stepfamilying, with its complicated households and living arrangements, means giving up even more control. There are the small matters, such as challenges to your time-honored "right" ways of cooking. There are the bigger ones, such as learning to work out compromises when you and your spouse differ on matters of discipline. Then there are the monster ones—like letting go of kids.

Letting go is separating your ego and your sense of identity from winning or losing. With kids and stepkids, it means that you discipline them based on what you believe to be best for them, not because it makes you feel powerful or because you need to win. It is seeing them as individuals who, with your guidance and support, will ultimately make their own choices. It means accepting the

103

things you cannot change instead of getting yourself tied up in knots trying to change something over which you have no control.

Letting go is an important part of good parenting for anyone. It's essential in a stepfamily. Sharing custody of kids, having kids move in and out of different households, and trying to define your role as a stepparent instead of a parent all make it necessary to practice letting go. Some parents simply can't handle losing that control. One mother had a fit when her son's stepmother volunteered to be a room parent at his elementary school. When his daughter chose to go live with her mother after spending three years with him, one father told her, "Fine, but if you go you aren't my daughter any more."

This man could have saved some heartache for himself and his daughter if he had been able to accept that one of the consequences of divorce is losing some control over your kids' lives. What goes on at your kids' and stepkids' other houses, short of actual abuse, is simply not any of your business. This isn't easy to take. It's hard to live with knowing that the kids may complain and moan about your rules, or their other parent may unfairly criticize you, and you won't be there to defend yourself. It's hard realizing that you aren't part of every bit of your kids' lives. It's hard to accept that you have no control over the relationship kids have with their other parents.

I have found it alternately discouraging and comforting, as the kids have grown older, to realize how little control we as parents or stepparents have over their long-term choices. Yes, parents can and should do their best to guide kids, teach them, and pass on values. But you don't have much to say about their basic personalities or the factors outside the family which affect them. The paradox is that, precisely because there is so much that is beyond your control, it's vital that you do your best with what you can influence.

It's important that you don't confuse letting go with giving up. It does not mean abandoning discipline or letting kids run the household. This has been a source of much of the ongoing conflict

I've had over the years with Stephanie. She has accused me bitterly more than once of being manipulating and controlling. What hasn't ever made sense to her is that parents are supposed to have more say than kids do and are supposed to have some control over kids' behavior. Setting limits and boundaries, enforcing rules, and expecting certain standards of behavior isn't being controlling, it's being a parent. You need to let go of your kids and stepkids, not your authority.

Knowing when to let go and what to let go of is a constant struggle. If you battle with your stepson over cleaning his room, are you being a responsible parent or a control freak? If you won't let your stepdaughter take her little brother shopping because he has homework to do, are you taking care of his needs or just being difficult because you want to annoy her? If you say goodbye to your kids cheerfully when they move to their other parent's house, are you heartless and uncaring or are you letting go? Nobody can answer such questions except you—and most of the time, you can't answer them, either. All you can do is remember the Serenity Prayer, try to act with your heart more than your ego, and do the best you can.

You can also concentrate on the rewards of letting go. Some of them are direct and practical. When you share parenting, you give up some control but you get a break from the day-to-day responsibility. Your kids and stepkids get the benefit of having more parents who can care about them and teach them from different perspectives. Your life is more comfortable when you don't have to hold on tightly and be in control of everything around you.

Some of the rewards are less tangible. The real blessing in learning to let kids go comes in realizing that genuine love doesn't have to hold on to someone. Instead, it gives kids the freedom to love and learn from someone besides yourself. It lets them go freely and welcomes them back the same way. Real love is offered with open hearts and open hands. It is letting go of what was never yours to hold onto in the first place.

105

Eight

Former Spouses

Just plain old parenting is a challenge. Parenting kids and stepkids in a blended family is even more difficult. But it gets really complicated when you add in all the other parents who are in there getting in your way. If you have kids, your spouse has kids, and both your former spouses have remarried, that's a total of six parents and stepparents involved at various levels with various combinations of kids. That means six different parenting styles, theories, and opinions. Then factor in the all-too-common complications such as conflicts with former spouses over money, visitation, lifestyles, what's best for the kids, who was right or wrong in the divorce, etcetera, etcetera, etcetera. And we wonder why stepfamilies are so difficult.

Our stepfamily has been fortunate when it comes to former spouses. Dean and his former wife, Jeri, went through that rarity, an amicable divorce, and they get along well now. She and I also are comfortable with one another—a brief phone call about what time to pick up the kids might turn into a half-hour chat about not only the kids but several other interests we have in common. Jeri, her husband Byron, Dean, and I are basically in agreement a lot of the time about parenting decisions and do a reasonably good job of supporting rather than undermining one another. When there is any conflict, Dean and Jeri are able to deal with the issues involved and focus on solving the problem rather than getting tangled up in blaming or jealousy or power struggles.

The other side of the family isn't quite so great. My former husband and I were not on anything even approaching comfortable terms for six or seven years after our divorce. For a long time Gary was still as angry, hurt, and bitter as he was the day I left. We weren't able to discuss what was best for Loren and Rachel, visitation, anything about one another's lives, or money. We didn't communicate unless we had to, and then we were able to have civil conversations about his visiting the kids as long as we kept it short and limited to just the facts about times and places. That finally started changing a couple years ago. By now we can be at the same school event without tension, or we can talk for a few minutes if he calls or comes to pick up Rachel. I doubt that either of us would have the other on a list of "people I'd want along if I were stranded on a desert island," but we can interact comfortably enough. As far as I know, basically what brought about the change was simply the passing of time.

Whether you like them or hate them, welcome their involvement or wish they would fall off the ends of the earth, dealing with former spouses is a fact of life in a stepfamily. It will affect your parenting, your relationship with your spouse, your finances, and your living arrangements. So you might as well accept the reality of their presence and handle it as comfortably as you can.

The View From the High Road

For short-term comfort for the kids and long-term welfare for everyone, choose to be the one who is flexible and cooperative in dealing with former spouses. Be willing to adjust visitation schedules, holiday plans, and the like in whatever way seems best for the kids. In the short term, this may mean you feel at times as if you are being taken advantage of. In the long term, though, it will pay dividends in the form of your own peace of mind and the well-being of your children and stepchildren.

But what if you are as cooperative and flexible as you can be, and it still doesn't work? What if your ex-spouse is childish, petty, uncooperative, trashes you or your spouse to the kids, and tries to sabotage your parenting? Short of hiring a hit man or changing your name and leaving town, what can you do?

Not a whole heck of a lot. You can't control someone else's actions. You can't make someone else be mature, nice, or reasonable. The only thing you can do is manage your own attitude. It's worthwhile to work at this if for no other reason than your own serenity.

1. Try to remember that, where the kids are concerned, you're all on the same side. You may differ in the best way to go about it, but most likely you all want the kids to grow up to be functional, happy adults who pay their bills and stay out of jail. Even if you think an ex-spouse is being stupid, obstructive, or incompetent, do your best to give them credit for good motives.

2. Remember that time is on your side. If problems with former spouses are due to bitterness over a divorce, they are likely to heal with time. And as kids grow up, your day-to-day involvement with the other parents will lessen.

3. Don't be holier than thou. You don't know what pain someone else might be dealing with or what's going on inside their head, so try not to judge or look down on them.

4. Remember that kids aren't stupid; they will figure out the truth for themselves when they are older and make their own assessments of their parents.

5. Always tell the truth—but not necessarily the whole truth. Some stuff is none of kids' business or not appropriate for them to know. The details of hassles with former spouses are in that category.

6. Keep your contact with a difficult ex-spouse businesslike and to a minimum. If phone calls tend to turn into shouting matches, for example, send a fax or a postcard.

7. Don't threaten to cut off contact with the kids or use time with them as a weapon. It hurts the kids far more than anyone else.

8. Don't give up on discipline with the kids because you're trying too hard not to be the bad guy. This isn't a competition for

"good guy of the year." If a former spouse over-indulges the kids or lets them run wild, it's even more important for you to be a responsible parent. It may seem as if the kids love the lax parent better, but in reality they respect a parent who sets limits. It's your job to be a good parent, not to be the best-liked adult in the kids' lives.

9. Settle for what you get in terms of cooperation from ex-spouses instead of wasting energy fussing over what you don't get. Sometimes the most constructive path is to shut up, make the best of things, and put your efforts into getting on with your own life.

10. Never, ever, do it back. No matter how difficult ex-spouses are, don't ever criticize or complain about them to the kids. Don't try to make your kids or stepkids take sides, even if their other parent does. Vent your frustrations with your spouse or a support group, but never to the kids. They are entitled to establish their own truth about their other parent instead of having that relationship manipulated through your perspective.

Too Much of a Good Thing

It's tough having an unfriendly relationship with your former spouse. But having a friendly one can cause some hassles, too. Just ask Maggie.

Maggie's husband is proud of the fact that he has a good relationship with his ex-wife. Their divorce was without bitterness, and they amicably share custody of their two sons. Both Ted and Carolyn are flexible about schedules and visits, and they are able to talk comfortably about problems or concerns with the kids. So far so good. Maggie agrees that this friendly relationship makes life easier for everyone.

But sometimes she thinks Ted goes too far. Carolyn, who is not responsible about money, has several times asked Ted and Maggie for loans. She has always paid them back eventually, but usually later than she has promised and only after being reminded.

Ted has paid for repairs to Carolyn's car and her house. Once he even let her use his credit card when she went on a business trip. This bothers Maggie, but Ted doesn't see it as a problem.

Ted says his financial help for his ex-wife is just making sure his kids are being taken care of. Maggie thinks the child support he pays faithfully ought to be enough. They have had several arguments about this issue, and it's straining their marriage.

What makes a situation like this so difficult is that it isn't black and white. There isn't a clear line where Ted's financial responsibility for his children stops. He's right that letting his ex-wife struggle financially would make life harder for the kids. But Maggie's position makes sense, too. Carolyn's poor money management is no longer Ted's problem. Constantly bailing her out shouldn't be his job.

It gets even more complicated when you figure out that the real issue here for Maggie isn't money. She doesn't resent what Ted spends on his kids. She knows he is a responsible parent who cares very much for his boys, and she likes that about him. She does resent the money he gives or loans to Carolyn, however, not because of the money but because it feels as if he is putting his former marriage ahead of his current marriage. It makes her uncomfortable and uncertain about where his loyalty lies.

In this case, the beginning of a solution would be for Maggie to let Ted know about her fears. They need to talk about the underlying feelings, not argue about the money he gives to his ex-wife. If he is indeed still overly committed to his ex-wife, that's a starting point for Ted and Maggie to begin working to strengthen their marriage. If he is just thinking of what's best for his kids, then he and Maggie could begin to work together to figure out ways for the two of them to support the kids without Maggie feeling in second place.

Any time a partner appears to be overly involved with a former spouse, the question of loyalty comes up. That involvement can take various forms: financial support such as Ted gives Carolyn, taking care of home repairs, phone calls or meetings about problems other than those with the kids, celebrating birthdays or other holidays together. In some families, these actions might be perfectly comfortable and appropriate. In others, they could be a sign that someone still isn't emotionally finished with the former marriage. What matters most isn't the level of involvement but how people feel about it.

For a marriage to work, each partner has to feel like a high priority for the other. This is harder when stepfamilies and former spouses are part of the picture. It doesn't help to disregard financial responsibilities or try to pretend the emotional ties to former spouses don't exist. But it's crucial for both partners in the new marriage to make clear that their primary loyalty is to each other.

Gossip

For a while early in our stepfamilying, Stephanie kept meticulous account of all the ways I was mean to her little brother. Any time I disciplined Peter, she would give me a look intended to freeze me in my tracks. Later I would hear her on the phone, giving her mother a play-by-play report of my most recent transgression. Fortunately, Jeri was wise enough not to play this game, and when she refused to get involved Stephanie eventually abandoned her attempts to get me into trouble.

This kind of household-to-household tattling isn't necessarily limited to young kids. A reader of my newspaper column a few years ago wrote about her grown stepchildren maliciously carrying information back and forth between their father's household and their mother's. Her question was, "How can I point out to the stepchildren that the only way their mother can hurt their father is through them? This is hurting them as well, since their gossiping causes their father to distance himself from them."

It was likely in this case that the children already knew they were hurting their father—and that's exactly what they intended because of leftover resentment from the divorce or other conflicts in the family. In a situation like this with adult children, it would certainly be appropriate for the father, not the stepmother, to confront them about their behavior.

But a deeper issue around gossip is accepting the difficult truth that we can't control another person's actions. If children, grown or not, are going to tell Mom what goes on at Dad's house and vice versa, we really can't do much about it. Yes, it's possible to tell children, "Don't say anything about this." But that puts them unfairly in a position of being asked to keep secrets and take sides between parents.

So what can you do about the problem of tale-bearing between families? You can try to find a balance—using enough common sense to protect yourself if necessary, but not tangling yourself up in secrecy and paranoia. It's sensible not to confide details of your finances, job worries, or a conflict with your spouse to kids or stepkids. Even if you don't care whether that information is passed on, it's not really their business. You need to find adult friends to talk to and get support from.

And you can choose not to waste a lot of energy wondering what someone might tell someone else about you. You can confront gossips if they are old enough and if their behavior is causing you pain. You can ignore them if it isn't. You can make sure you aren't guilty of tale-bearing yourself by choosing not to question our kids about their other parents. And, perhaps most important, you can decide to accept yourself as less than perfect.

Living in a blended family is a challenging situation with more than its share of stress and conflict. You aren't always going to do everything right—as your kids, stepkids, and former spouses will be happy to point out. Kids or stepkids who are angry at you will be quick to pass along your failings to their other parents. Their accusations or reports will be the most painful when they have a grain of truth in them.

It wasn't hard for me to ignore Stephanie's reports about my horrible treatment of Peter, because I was confident that I wasn't really treating him badly. It was much harder when my kids passed on some information to their father and he attacked me about some things which I could have done better. I first had to admit to myself that I had made some mistakes and that his accusations were partially true, instead of staying in a position of defending myself and pretending I had been perfect. Only then did the gossip lose its power to hurt, and only then was I able to let go of the part of it which was exaggerated.

It also helps to remember that the other parent isn't going to be perfect, either. Your household isn't the only one which has stresses, mistakes, and conflicts. While you're admitting your own mistakes to yourself, give yourself some room to forgive the other parents for theirs. This isn't a competition. You're all just flawed human beings in difficult situations, trying to do your best. So it's a good idea to decide not to believe everything you hear—good or bad—about the other household.

In many cases, if you don't worry about gossip it will fizzle out because of lack of response. Your best choice is often to do the best you can in your own stepfamily, acknowledge that nobody will do everything perfectly, and mind your own business. Then you can let others manage their own behavior and let any gossip go harmlessly on by.

Extended Families

When Loren was 13, he faced a challenge in writing a thank-you note to Dean's father for a Christmas gift when the two of them hadn't even met yet. He finally started his letter with, "Dear (ahem) Grandpa John." That "ahem" was his way of compromising between the too-familiar "Grandpa" and the too-formal "Mr."

Loren's dilemma is typical of the situations we find ourselves in as we try to fit blended families into extended families. We don't marry in isolation. In addition to children and ex-spouses, each of us is part of a family that may include parents, brothers and sisters, nephews and nieces, aunts and uncles and cousins. Our relatives certainly don't have the right to control our choices about marriage, but they are affected to some degree by what we do. So how does our new blended family fit into our old extended family? Or does it even need to?

An unexpected gift for me with my second marriage was the matter-of-fact acceptance of my children by my husband's mother. She simply added two more grandchildren to her Christmas list, wrote down their birthdates and measurements, and carried on. As well as being a bonus for my kids (after all, anybody can use one more grandparent), it felt like a validation of my place in that family as her new daughter-in-law.

Unfortunately, it isn't always that simple. Parents may be attached to their son or daughter's former spouse and resent a new daughter- or son-in-law. Perhaps they feel as if they've lost their grandchildren if the former in-law has custody. That might create resentment of step-grandchildren. Or maybe they just plain don't feel like being grandma or grandpa to kids who already have grandparents of their own.

Stepchildren, too, aren't necessarily going to be overwhelmed with delight at the prospect of a new set of grandparents, aunts, uncles, and cousins. Being told some strange woman they've never met is their new Aunt Susan probably won't get much response beyond "Oh, yeah?" unless Aunt Susan is a celebrity or shows up laden with presents.

So what's the best thing to do about relationships with extended family members? Most of the time, nothing. This is a good time to practice letting go of expectations. You chose this spouse and this blended family. Your parents didn't, your siblings didn't, your children didn't (as they probably remind you from time to time). Don't expect to create instant grandparent/grandchild bonding. Don't assume your brother will want to become "Uncle Dave" overnight to your stepchildren, complete with invitations to fishing trips or birthday presents or summer jobs. Just step back and let everybody get to know each other in their own way.

If some relatives have resentments or are slow to welcome your new family, remember it isn't your job to change them. Do speak up—to your spouse first—if someone seems to be treating children with blatant unfairness or an intent to hurt them. You don't have to tolerate grandparents taking their own hurt over a divorce out on children who are innocent third parties. But don't work too hard to turn all these people into an instant family. Keep the lines of communication open, but don't push everybody to form relationships they may not be ready for. Close relationships may develop, and that's wonderful. Or they may not, and that's fine, too. Either way, your priority is the relationships within your own stepfamily.

Do stay open-minded and flexible when you deal with extended families. Save room if you can for some compassion for the difficult position grandparents can find themselves in. You don't have to force relationships, but be sure you aren't standing in their way, either. Being open to all kinds of grandparent and step-grandparent options can lead to an extended family circle which enriches everyone involved.

Nine

Getting the Message—
Effective Communication

You Can't Fix It If You Don't Talk About It

Early in our stepfamilying, Dean's kids were spending a summer weekend with us. A short time before we were due to take them back to their mother's house, Jeri called. The message she left with Stephanie, who answered the phone, was that she wouldn't be home until later than the time we had planned to drop the kids off. What Dean and I understood was that we should keep the kids at our house until later. What Stephanie understood was that it was okay for them to go to their mom's and that she would see them when she got home. Cause—simple miscommunication. Result—large battle. When arguing and shouting didn't convince us that Stephanie's version of the message was the right one, she finally slammed out the door and marched off down the street in a dramatic huff with her suitcase, her pillow, and her hairdryer.

Over the years, we've had countless miscommunications of this nature. Some of them have been trivial, some of them have been funny, and some of them have blown up into major conflicts. Many of them could have been avoided had someone just been able to communicate more clearly in the first place.

I am waiting impatiently for human beings to evolve to the point where we can communicate by mental telepathy. It would be so much easier. Unfortunately, I'm beginning to think that won't happen in my lifetime. And, if I stop to think about it, maybe it's just as well that the kids sometimes don't know what I'm thinking.

(I already know there are times when I'm better off not knowing what they're thinking.)

So since we can't transfer our intentions directly into someone else's brain, it's important to work harder at getting messages across with the tools we already have. As one of the adults in the stepfamily, it's up to you to set an example of clear communication. Some of the ways you can start might include:

1. Make arrangements for visitation, such as picking kids up, directly with the other parents, not through the kids. In the previous example, we could have spared ourselves an uproar—and saved Stephanie a hike with her suitcase—had either Dean or I talked directly to Jeri.

2. Remember that an unspoken contract isn't an agreement with anyone except yourself. I have a habit of making one-sided bargains in my head. If I take the kids out for lunch on Saturday, then they should be happy to help me clean the garage when we get home. There's nothing wrong with an arrangement like that; the problem comes when I don't communicate it to the kids. Then I get resentful because they aren't keeping their part of the agreement, and they get angry because they didn't know they were making an agreement.

3. Communicate with the right person. Don't expect your kids to carry messages to your ex-spouse about unpaid child support or the orthodontics they need; it isn't their responsibility. Don't chew your stepson out because your spouse let him do something you didn't agree with; talk to your spouse instead.

4. Realize that sometimes you will need to dig for information. Kids are fuzzy about minor little details like what time they are supposed to be at softball practice or when their science report is due. You may need to keep asking questions, have them look up a due date, or make a phone call to find out what you need to know. You are the adult; it's your job to make sure that necessary information is communicated.

5. Accept as a fact that all kids will sometimes lie. Lying, for younger kids, often seems to be the easiest way out of a

predicament. "Yes, I practiced my spelling words." "No, I didn't take Tyler's pack of gum." They haven't learned yet that lying is dumb as well as wrong, because in the long run the consequences are worse. This doesn't mean you should tolerate lying. Nor is it useful to assume that kids are always being untruthful. Just keep it in the back of your mind as a possibility. Especially when two kids in the household are in the middle of a conflict, be aware that their respective versions of the facts will be carefully edited in their own favor.

6. Always tell the truth. Clear communication starts with honesty, and you can't expect that from kids if you don't practice it yourself. If you're taking a small child to the doctor for a shot, don't say it won't hurt. Say, "It will hurt a little, but it will be over with right away." If you threw away a toy because it was left in the middle of the living room for three days and got stepped on and broken, don't say you don't know where it is. Kids don't always need the whole truth in four-part harmony with all the details, but they do deserve to be told the truth. If they ask about something that you don't think they should know, you have every right to tell them politely that it isn't their business or you don't want to talk about it.

7. Remember that the goal of communication is to share information and understand one another better. Save the interrogations, accusations, and verbal tricks for the courtroom. Do your best to stay on the same side rather than setting up an adversarial situation.

Communicating clearly and effectively takes continued effort. It demands your presence, your attention, and your energy. Yet, as I look back on our stepfamilying so far, I have to conclude that the vast majority of our hassles have been at least partly because of poor communication. Investing some energy in learning to communicate more effectively is well worth everything it takes. It's a critical factor in building a successful stepfamily.

It's Not Just What You Say, It's How You Say It

Try an experiment with the people around you for the next few days. When someone is talking, concentrate on their inflection and tone of voice instead of what they are saying. You might want to choose your conversations carefully here. Tuning out some instructions from your boss or a reminder from one of the kids about picking them up for gymnastics practice could have consequences.

It's easy to hear the inflection most people use to talk to babies or toddlers. It's an "aren't you cute?" tone that most of us seem to adopt automatically (though some people take it to nauseating extremes). But if you pay attention, you might be surprised at the different tones you can pick up or at the messages they convey.

Listen to the way members of your family talk to each other. Are older kids curt or teasing with younger ones? Who whines, and when? Do people give orders or make requests when they ask for food to be passed at the dinner table? Can you tell who someone is talking to on the phone by their voice? Stephanie used to have one telephone voice for friends, another one for her mother, and a third for people she babysat for.

After you've had some practice in noticing other people's inflections comes the hard part. Start paying attention to your own. Do you have different voices for your spouse and your kids? Your boss and the waitress at the cafe where you eat lunch? Your mother and your mother-in-law? Your kids and your stepkids? If you have the courage to do it, leaving a tape recorder running while you're at the dinner table can be eye-opening.

Notice particularly whether you have different tones for your children and your stepchildren. You might be using the identical words, but if you tend to sound pleasant with your kids and irritated with your stepkids, you're sending an unmistakable message about who comes first in the family.

Several years ago a couple I knew started the process of adopting a little boy just a month before the wife gave birth to a baby. As she struggled with the stress of suddenly becoming the parent of a newborn and a toddler, Cindy wasn't able to manage loving both of them. It was appalling to hear her coo sweetly at her baby daughter and then snap harshly at the boy. Fortunately for him, the adoption process was stopped and he was placed in another family.

Pay particular attention to differences in adults' voices (including your own) when they talk to other adults and when they talk to kids. One day I was in a store and overhead the manager on the phone. She was chewing somebody out in a tone that said, "you are so stupid and don't you talk back to me." It made me cringe, and I thought, "Thank goodness I don't work for somebody who treats her employees like that."

Then I realized she was talking to one of her kids. And my first reaction was, "Oh, that's okay then." Which appalled me when I thought about it. Because it isn't okay. Most of us wouldn't think it acceptable to be so rude to another adult. Why should it be okay to do so with kids?

When some new neighbors moved in across the street a few years ago, the wife warned me, "I'm a screamer." And she certainly was. We could hear her in the summertime, letting her kids have it in a voice you could have used for sandpaper. Even if she wasn't scolding them, her voice made it clear that she was expecting them to misbehave any minute and when they did, they'd get exactly what was coming to them. The whole block relaxed a notch when the family moved away.

The problem with a harsh tone of voice isn't merely that it's unkind. It also isn't useful. Talking to kids in a tone that says, "You are stupid and bad and you irritate me beyond belief" creates a whole lot of resentment. It sends a message that you don't like them. It comes across as an attack. It builds an atmosphere of tension instead of cooperation.

Please don't misunderstand this to mean you should always talk to your kids in a "sweet little darling" tone of voice. I know a couple of people who do that, and it comes across as incredibly phony. If your teenager has stayed out past curfew and didn't call and you're really angry, you don't want to sound nice. What you do want is to have your tone of voice match the circumstances. If you're mad, be congruently mad or you won't sound real. But save your mad voice for the times you have reason to use it. If you use it all the time, the kids won't pay any attention when you really are angry.

When you start listening to your own inflections, you might not be pleased at some of the things you hear. I know I catch myself much too often talking to the kids in a voice that says, "When are you ever going to grow up and get civilized?"

It is certainly possible to change your inflections if you find you are using some that are too harsh. The way to do it is not easy, but it's simple—you practice. After all, this is something all of us know how to do already. If you stop and pay attention, you'll realize how often you already change your tone of voice to a more pleasant one. It's helpful for me to remember those times when I want to change the way I talk to my kids. You might find some of the following strategies useful:

1. When I'm in a grumpy mood and my business phone rings, before I answer it I stop and take a breath so I can sound pleasant. I switch gears instead of letting my irritation contaminate what I say on the phone. I already know how to do this with my customers. I can practice the same thing with my family.

2. Relax your face and smile before you talk. A simple, "Here's the laundry that you need to fold," can sound entirely different when you're frowning than it does when you're smiling. If you're brave enough, practice this one in front of a mirror.

3. Remember to suggest and ask rather than give orders. A request with a "please" in it can still come out in a "you stupid kid" tone, of course. But it improves your chances of sounding pleasant if you word your sentences in a courteous way.

4. Pretend you have company. If television news cameras were rolling or friends were visiting, you'd be able to put forth

enough extra effort to sound pleasant. So that means you can do the same even when no one is around but family.

5. Remember the power of being pleasantly matter-of-fact. I'm always impressed when I go into a well-managed elementary classroom. The teachers are able to maintain a comfortable sense of order and make it look easy. There will be a herd of 20 or 25 kids, sometimes all busy with separate projects, sometimes working together on something. When they're finishing, the teacher says, "All right, it's time to pick things up and get ready for the next class." And they do it—quickly and cheerfully. It amazes me. How in the world do they do that?

One of the techniques I've noticed good teachers use is pleasant matter-of-factness. They don't blame or scold or accuse. They simply assume everyone will do what they're supposed to. They give the kids a message that of course they will cooperate, and most of the time the kids do. This pleasant expectation of good behavior goes a long way toward building cooperation.

Actions Speak Louder Than Words

One of my most embarrassing memories as a parent is an incident that happened when Rachel was four. She and her brother were fighting, and she hit him with a book. I grabbed her, gave her several swats on the backside, and shouted, "You don't hit people!"

The incongruity of that hit me much harder than she had hit her brother—and convinced me that spanking isn't usually an appropriate disciplinary tool. If I tell my kids one thing but do another, they'll remember what I do much more than what I say.

If you call in sick when you're perfectly well but you want the day off, how can you legitimately tell your kids not to lie? When you complain to your daughter about your stepdaughter's bad habits, how can you credibly tell her she should emphasize the positive things about her stepsister? When you scream at your kids and stepkids, how can you look them in the eye and tell them to be courteous to each other?

A huge amount of what you communicate to your kids and stepkids is nonverbal. I remember a man in a support group talking about his difficult relationship with his teenage son, who was in juvenile detention at the time for attacking his father. The father said, "I know I don't abuse him. I never hit him except when he has it coming. And I make sure I tell him every night that I love him." Obviously, the boy paid more attention to the beatings than to the words.

You can't transmit what you know to your kids by telling them. It simply doesn't work that way. You have spent years struggling toward maturity and trying to grow up. How can you possibly expect your kids to get to the same place you are just because you tell them what you know? They can't hear it. They have to do it. And they learn how to do it by watching how you do it.

Yes, you need to pass on your values and beliefs, and part of that comes from telling kids what you think is important. But it matters much more that they see you living out those values. Pay more attention to your actions than your words—they have far louder voices.

Random Acts of Communication

In one of her columns, Erma Bombeck said that for years the only conversations she had with her kids were shouted through bathroom doors. A lot of that goes on at our house, too. There's something about a parent behind a locked door which brings out a child's urge to communicate. (Usually something like, "But I have to leave for school in five minutes and I need my gym clothes washed or I'm going to get a zero!")

In contrast are the occasions when we as parents feel the need for some Meaningful Communication with a child. We set aside

123

time, sit them down for a heart-to-heart talk, and what do we get? As likely as not, nothing. "How do you feel about that?" "I dunno." "What's going on with this?" "Nothin'."

Real communication doesn't happen when parents are preoccupied with their own affairs most of the time, then have periodic attacks of guilt and swoop down on the kids to have Intimate Talks About Serious Issues. It happens when you make yourself available on a regular basis. Meaningful conversations, like many other things, don't happen by accident. They take place when an atmosphere to nurture and promote them has been created. It's especially important in a stepfamily to create such a climate.

The first step in that direction is simply arranging to be around when kids have something to say.

In elementary school, Peter was the first one of our kids home from school. He would come charging into the house, and his first words were inevitably, "What's for snack?" So I would get out his snack, and usually I would hang around the kitchen while he demolished it. Through mouthfuls of cake or graham cracker, he would start to talk. "Know what happened today? We were playing soccer at recess, you know? And it was so windy, that guess what? The ball was just sitting there, and the wind blew it in for a goal, and our side won!"

I would find out quite a bit about Peter and what was happening in school in the ten or fifteen minutes before Amy and Rachel came home. Then it would be their turn, and somewhat the same thing would happen in stereo as they both filled me in about the happenings in fifth or sixth grade.

Now if I would be on the phone when they came home, or too busy at the computer to take a break, or out at a customer's, I would miss out on those conversations. The kids were usually primed to talk when they got home, and if nobody was there to talk to, the moment would pass. Dean and I could find out about their respective days at the dinner table if we made the effort to ask, but we would usually need to initiate the conversation.

Now that the kids are older and more involved with their friends and activities outside the family, they aren't quite as ready to talk. But over the years we have created a habit of communication around "What's for snack?" and "So how was school today?" Because of that pattern, we often still have some good conversations when they get home.

Conversations with kids happen when you least expect them, at odd moments throughout the day. If you aren't there to take advantage of those random acts of communication, it's hard to get them started later. One undeniable fact about fostering communication is that it requires your time and your presence. I'm fortunate in being self-employed and able to arrange my schedule so I'm usually there when the kids get home from school. A lot of parents don't have that luxury. If both you and your spouse have full-time jobs, making time for communication is tougher. It takes a commitment of energy that you aren't always going to want to make.

But keep in mind that quality time for communicating with others in the family is something to nurture rather than force. The idea isn't to add "spend time talking with kids" as another chore on your already busy schedule. Instead, take a look at the things you already do with your time and think about some ways you might be able to make changes or include kids in your activities.

For example:

1. Are people in your family in the habit of turning on the TV as soon as they get home? What would happen if you left it off unless there was a specific program that someone really wanted to watch? Television is the king of conversation-killers. If it has become a mindless habit at your house, you might want to examine your family's viewing patterns and make some changes. Computer games or time on-line can be just as bad. Both these technologies can be great ways to learn something or be entertained. Just make sure you're using them in appropriate and limited ways. And kids absolutely don't need TV sets or computers in their bedrooms to encourage them to isolate themselves.

2. Invite one kid at a time along when you go shopping or run errands. Two people in a car is a great opportunity for conversation. Going for a walk is even better. Dean and I have most of our significant talks when we're walking, out of the house and away from interruptions.

3. Do household chores together. Before we had a dishwasher, the kids would take turns washing while Dean or I rinsed. We usually had a pleasant time with the designated dishwasher; there's something about standing together at the sink that generates conversation. You can have the whole family do chores together (maybe you could clean house on Saturday mornings and then go out to lunch to reward yourselves), or you can pair up with different kids on household projects.

4. Make family mealtimes a priority. When everyone gets together regularly around the dinner table, communication tends to get passed around along with the mashed potatoes or the salad. Obviously, this isn't going to be possible all the time in a busy family with conflicting schedules. But do what you can to have the family at least eat dinner together as often as you can. It's important family-building time.

Making yourself available for random acts of communication is especially helpful if you would like to build closer bonds with your stepchildren. When you do have opportunities to communicate with stepkids, don't push. Don't expect to instantly get into heavy issues or resolve tensions. Building trust and a level of comfort takes time. You might start out by talking about who won the football game or what happened in school. The idea is to open a channel and start building the habit of communication over small things, so that eventually you can talk about the bigger stuff.

Listening

One day when Peter was four, he came home from preschool and burst through the kitchen door. He wrapped himself around my leg and said urgently, "Guess what! Know what happened today?"

This sounded important. I squatted down in my best "attentive parent" mode to hear his news. "What happened?"

"Today Christopher—you know what? He picked his nose, and it bled!"

So much for deep heart-to-heart communication. But it was important news to Peter right at that minute. And he needed me to listen right at that minute.

Listening doesn't necessarily take a lot of time. But it does require attention and effort. As you're working on better communication with your family, remember that listening is important, too. It is a powerful way of letting other people know you think they are important.

M. Scott Peck, M.D., in his book *The Road Less Traveled*, describes five different levels of responding when children talk. The one requiring the least effort is simply not allowing them to talk. The next easiest is letting them chatter as background noise, but tuning them out. The third is "pretend listening," where you don't really listen but you acknowledge their talking with "uh huh" or "oh" at what you hope might be appropriate places. The next level is "selective listening," where you tune out much of what a child says but stay alert enough to catch what seems important. The fifth and most difficult level, of course, is genuine listening. This is giving children your full attention and concentrating on what they say.

Peck points out that all of these methods have their place. Sometimes you do need to have kids be quiet. Tuning out or pretend listening are often perfectly adequate for chattering small children, who get the attention they need through your presence more than your ears. Selective listening is a valuable strategy that most parents use a lot. Then there are times when kids urgently need genuine, effortful listening. The crucial part of good parental listening is recognizing those times.

Listening is like any other skill. The more you practice it, the better you'll get. So when you have some time with a kid, don't spend all of it with your mouth open. Practice being available and ready to listen.

But what if you're doing your best to make time and space available for communication, you're all primed and attentive and ready to listen—and the kid won't say anything?

Well, you could ask a few questions to get things started, as long as you don't turn a talk into an interrogation. Make them open-ended questions that can't be answered with yes or no, then do your best to build on them with comments of your own rather than just asking another question. Or you could just be quiet for a while and see what happens. As long as it's friendly, there's certainly nothing wrong with a little silence. And give it time. Don't expect an instant flood of communication just because you're prepared to listen. Maybe today all you'll get is a couple of two-word answers. The next time, and the next, you might get a little more, until a habit of conversation gets established.

One key to listening, especially with older kids, is to communicate respectfully in the same way you would with another adult. Don't interrupt them. Don't laugh at or belittle their opinions. (How sophisticated were your beliefs when you were ten or fifteen?) Don't ask a question and then ignore the answer.

Another key to genuine listening is to get past the "how" of a message and pay attention to the "what." If an angry child is shouting at you, one choice would be to disregard the shouting and respond to the content. This doesn't mean it's okay to let kids scream at you or allow yourself to be verbally abused. You can say something like, "I understand this is important, and we'll talk about it, but I won't discuss it while you're calling me names." But sometimes kids shout because it feels like the only way to get someone's attention. If they learn that they will be heard, they will eventually figure out that they don't have to shout.

Remember that listening to a child doesn't mean feeling obligated to come up with a solution to a problem. Sometimes the

128

listening is all you need to do. Terry Kellogg, who presents workshops on parenting, suggests a useful slogan: Just say, "Oh." When a child comes to you in despair because she spent all her allowance on candy and has no money for the weekend, just say, "Oh." When your stepson says accusingly that his real mom or dad would never be so unfair, just say "Oh." (It's fun to try it with different inflections—just be careful not to be sarcastic.) He offers this as almost a joke, but the core message of it is a terrific tool. You don't have to answer every accusation, solve every problem, or respond to every complaint. Sometimes all children need is an acknowledgment that you heard them.

Good listening doesn't have to mean changing your mind or letting a kid argue forever, either. You may have listened carefully, considered their point of view, and still said, "No." It's perfectly okay after a certain point to say, "Enough is enough. I'm not going to discuss this any more."

Listening is a two-way street, of course. Because nothing drives me to screaming incoherence faster than feeling I am being ignored, I would love to find a magic potion that could get kids to listen. I try to remember that all children suffer from an ailment called "Intermittent Selective Deafness." A child in the living room will hear perfectly well when you, in the kitchen, say something softly to your spouse about ice cream. That same child, ten minutes later, will not hear you when you shout, "Please remember to take out the garbage before you leave!"

Because of this disease, it's helpful to make sure you have a child's attention before you say something important. Don't do it while they're in the middle of a computer game or a favorite television show. Don't make a habit of shouting from another room. Touch them, say their name, or make eye contact to be sure you have established a connection before you start talking. If you need to give complicated instructions ("Put the casserole in the oven at 5:00 at 350 degrees, then make a salad and set the table."), have the listener repeat back what you just said.

As always, of course, the most powerful teaching is by example. It's unreasonable to expect kids not to interrupt if you constantly interrupt them. It's unfair to turn what is supposed to be a discussion into a lecture. If kids know you will listen to them when it's their turn to talk, they're more likely to grant you the same courtesy.

The Family Meeting

Many books on parenting recommend family meetings. Most parents I know think they're a good idea. Most parents I know, myself included, don't use them.

Why not? Maybe it's too much hassle to get everybody together regularly. Maybe starting something new and different takes more energy than we have right now. Maybe we don't know how to go about it. Or maybe we're afraid it will mean giving up parental control.

Whatever the reasons, those of us who don't use family meetings might be missing out on a valuable tool for fostering harmony and cooperation. If you'd like to consider trying them at your house, here are some suggestions which might help get you started. (Some of the following ideas come from Chapter 8 of *Perfect Parenting & Other Myths*, by Dr. Frank Main (Prairie Flower Press). This book is a good source for additional information.)

1. Bring up the idea of family meetings as a suggestion rather than an order. If some family members aren't excited about the idea, perhaps they would agree to three or four meetings on a trial basis.

2. Schedule meetings at a regular time and place that's neutral ground. Just getting together in the living room is perfectly fine. Or you could all go out for breakfast on Saturday mornings or for ice cream one evening a week, which might give reluctant family members some incentive to give the meetings a try. Just make sure

everyone knows you're getting together specifically for a meeting; it won't work to try to turn a family outing into a meeting when that isn't what people are expecting.

3. Be open and flexible at first about your goals and format. Let the family as a group decide ways to be sure everyone has a turn to speak, how often and how long to meet, and what topics will be included. Some regular discussion items might include chores, conflicts, schedules, vacations, and finances.

4. Keep in mind that your purposes are more important than the specific ways you work toward them. Purposes for your meetings might include making decisions, fostering cooperation, assigning chores fairly, resolving conflicts, etc. As long as everyone knows what those goals are, you can be flexible about changing your format as your family needs change.

6. Rotate the job of chairing the meeting, with this role being to keep everyone on track rather than to make decisions or guide the discussion.

7. Keep the meeting pleasant and positive. Establish some guidelines at the beginning to help people express their opinions without trashing someone else. And it's best to make decisions through consensus rather than voting, so you don't have "winners" and "losers."

8. To have a genuine family meeting, it's important that everyone be involved. But what if someone in the family refuses to participate? If others are interested, you could start meetings anyway. Otherwise the family is letting that one person dictate to all of them. The first meetings might include figuring out ways to fairly include the non-participant in assigned chores or other decisions that affect the whole family. At the same time, you wouldn't want to use the meetings to punish or isolate that person. It would probably be most useful for the rest of the family to go matter-of-factly about the family business, making it clear that the non-participant is welcome to join at any time but not begging or urging them.

131

If the uninvolved person is a parent, it might mean limiting the scope of meetings. After all, it wouldn't be realistic to make family vacation plans without Dad. But it still could be useful to start meetings, even if they cover a smaller territory.

If two or more people don't want to participate, it probably isn't the right time for family meetings at your house. Perhaps you could begin to establish a pattern of making more decisions through family discussions, and bring up the idea of formal meetings again later.

One circumstance where family meetings could do more harm than good would be in a blended family where one side of the family wants to have meetings and the other doesn't. In this case, if Dad and his kids start meetings without Mom and her kids, it's likely to divide the family rather than help build cooperation.

9. If you as a parent aren't willing to at least try the idea of letting kids participate in decisions, family meetings aren't going to work. If a "meeting" is just a place for parents to lecture or assign chores, there's no point in having one.

This doesn't mean that starting family meetings is turning over all the decisions or power to the kids. It's perfectly okay to have some limits on what can be decided at the meetings. For example, menus might be open for discussion as long as they provide for balanced meals and show consideration for the budget and the cook. Decisions about curfews or use of the family car might be made separately from family meetings. Some parents might be more comfortable keeping veto power in some areas; just be sure that is spelled out clearly in the beginning.

10. Remember that family meetings, like families, don't have to be perfect in order to be valuable. The mere fact that you get together regularly to discuss family issues can be enormously useful.

Family meetings can help give everyone in the family a sense of ownership in decisions. Successful family meetings give each person, adult or child, a chance to be heard. This can build a spirit of cooperation and shared responsibility.

Ten

The Untouchable Issue—
Money

Money can be a touchy subject in any family. Spouses may come into a marriage with unequal earnings, separate debts, different spending and saving habits, and different core beliefs about money—all of which can cause conflict and stress. If couples are remarrying, they bring along added "stuff" from their former marriages. Maybe one of the reasons for Sarah's divorce was her ex-husband's financial irresponsibility, and she is afraid to share money management with her new husband. Maybe Dan thinks he got taken to the cleaners by his ex-wife, so he is reluctant to trust his new wife with his money or property. And that's even before factoring in all the other financial issues in a blended family: financial obligations or entanglements with former spouses, paying or receiving child support, providing fairly for everyone's children, partners with unequal incomes and assets, and complicated estate planning. Money can move in a hurry from a touchy subject to an untouchable one.

Because money is doubly hard to talk about in a blended family, it's essential to talk about it. Money issues are just as big a factor as child issues in destroying remarriages. You may start out with rosy optimism, sure that the money stuff will all work out. And maybe it will. But it's more likely to work out if you and your spouse work at it together.

Accept the Realities

When you commit to becoming part of a stepfamily, complicated and emotion-laden financial affairs are part of the package. Accepting that package means working within the limits and realities of your family's particular financial situation. Perhaps the budget is tighter than you wish it were. Perhaps you or your spouse have to pay alimony. Perhaps a former spouse tries to buy the kids' love with expensive gifts. Perhaps the child support you are supposed to receive doesn't always show up. Perhaps there simply doesn't seem to be enough cash to go around.

You don't have to like any of those things, but it will make your life easier if you accept their existence. Don't waste your energy by being a victim. You don't accomplish anything by resenting alimony payments or whining about a former spouse's financial irresponsibility or your current family's lack of money. Instead, go back to the Serenity Prayer. What can you change, and what do you need to accept? Alimony is probably in the category of things to accept. Inappropriate gifts or unpaid child support may or may not be things you can change. You can try discussing with your ex how harmful it is to try to buy kids' love. If nothing changes, at least you have done what you could. You can go to court over unpaid child support if you think that would be worthwhile. Or you can decide your chances of collecting any are so slim that you're better off planning to get along without it. The important thing is to make those choices based on the best information you have, then to accept the consequences of the choices and get on with your life.

If there just doesn't seem to be enough money to go around, change is certainly possible but might take some time and effort. The two basic ways to address the problem, of course, are to increase what comes in or decrease what goes out. In a stepfamily, it might be best to try hardest to decrease what goes out. Please don't ignore the fact that, for children, time is sometimes more important than money.

Maybe your household has four kids in it, your spouse works full time, and you work part-time. The obvious solution to money problems would seem to be for you to get a full-time job. But look at the implications thoroughly and carefully before you start updating your resume. The more time parents spend at work, the more stress is added to the family. If you both have to work full-time in order to buy shoes for the kids and put groceries on the table, then that's what you have to do. But make sure you really need to. It's more important for kids to have someone at home after school than it is for them to wear shoes with some overpaid athlete's name on them. It isn't necessarily even good for kids to have their own phone lines, TV sets in their rooms, high-end stereo systems, or expensive electronic games. The family doesn't have to take expensive vacations every year or eat out three or four times a week. Rummage-sale clothes and eight-year-old family cars are perfectly acceptable options. Pay attention to the priorities, and don't take time away from kids in order to buy them stuff that doesn't matter.

Our Kids, Not Yours and Mine

Is paying for your stepdaughter's orthodontia putting a strain on the family budget? Does it seem that every time you turn around, there is a stepkid with a hand out, needing yet more cash? Maybe you have accumulated a fund of nickel-and-dime irritations over small but annoying money issues. Or perhaps you have some major stuff about money in your stepfamily. This could be serious resentment because your spouse's ex isn't contributing and you are supporting someone else's kids. Or it might be grief and anger because you feel you can't afford to have a child of your own.

Let's face it, raising kids costs serious money. They need fed, they need clothed, they need allowances, they hurt themselves and need taken to the emergency room, they need gym shoes and school fees and braces on their teeth. And that's not even getting

135

into the question of the things they *want*. If you have kids of your own, you're probably used to this financial bottomless pit. If you don't, it can be appalling when you become a stepparent to watch the cash disappear. If that vanishing cash is yours, or if your stepkids' other parent isn't contributing, you can build up a fund of resentment in a hurry.

One of the most effective ways to end that resentment is to learn to think of all the kids in the family as "our kids" rather than "yours" and "mine." Then money for child support, dentists' bills, new shoes, and prom dresses is being spent on real people who are part of your life. The more you are involved with your stepkids, the less you will begrudge spending money for them.

If stepkids don't live in your household, and you don't know them very well, it's hard to feel generous about money that goes out on their behalf. You're not likely to become very enthusiastic about what you know primarily as a large budget item labeled "child support." The answer is still to become more involved with the kids.

It's harder to do this, of course, if kids aren't part of your household, but you can still work at it. You can go to basketball games and school conferences or become part of the car pool to ballet lessons. If the kids live a distance away, you can write and participate in phone calls. You can be a part of activities with them when they visit, rather than withdrawing and leaving everything up to your spouse. You don't have to invite yourself along on every single outing, but you can choose to think of their visits as family time, rather than time which takes your spouse away from you. Perhaps most important, you can encourage your spouse to stay involved with the kids and to talk about them, so you get into the habit of seeing them as important people in your spouse's life.

If stepkids live with you a significant part of the time, involvement with them happens more or less willy-nilly. Of course, it doesn't help much if they live with you and you can't stand them—which is why it's so important that you build bonds with stepkids as well as you can. If you are resentful because you are taking responsibility for someone else's child support obligation, it may help to practice some long-term thinking. It might not matter much to the kids right now who is paying for their new shoes and their contact lenses, but chances are they will appreciate it when they're older. ("Older" in this case probably means about 35.) It also helps to concentrate on what you are gaining and what the kids' non-paying parent is losing. Many times a parent who doesn't pay child support is also less involved in children's lives in other ways. This means that when you choose to assume financial responsibility for your stepkids, you also have the opportunity to be there for them in other significant ways and to build closeness with them that can enrich your life as well as theirs.

Day-to-Day Management

How do you and your spouse manage money? Do you dump everything into one pot or divide up expenses and income into "his" and "hers" pots? Do you make all decisions jointly? Do you each have some separate spending money of your own? Does the person earning the most money make most of the financial decisions?

Here are some ways remarried couples manage their finances:

1. Anne and Mike both work and earn average salaries; his is about a third more than hers. Mike has no children; Anne has custody of her two children. She puts her paycheck and her child support checks into her account. He puts his paycheck into his account. They each are responsible for certain household bills, divided up in proportion to their income. Other than paying those bills, they don't have to account to each other for what they spend. They plan large purchases and investments together.

2. Aaron has three children from his former marriage; Melissa has not been married before. His children live with their mother and visit their father on weekends and during the summer. Both Aaron and Melissa have high incomes from professional jobs, and both have separate investments and property from before their marriage. They each deposit their paychecks into their separate accounts and then pay equal shares into a joint household account. Aaron pays child support, alimony, and his personal expenses from his account; household expenses are paid from the joint account; and Melissa pays her personal expenses and makes her car payment from her account. They plan major purchases relating to the house or other joint projects together; they keep their investments separated and make separate decisions on major individual purchases such as cars.

3. Karen and Walt have been married for five years. His three children live with them half the time; her one child lives with them all the time, and she receives no child support from her ex-husband. Walt earns a substantial salary; Karen earns about one-sixth as much from a part-time job. Both their incomes go into one account. Karen pays all the bills and handles finances as part of her responsibilities as the household manager. Each of them has an equal weekly cash allowance as "walking-around money" that doesn't have to be accounted for to the other. They consult each other on major purchases, though Karen defers to Walt's wishes because he earns most of the money.

These different styles are based on different stepfamilies' needs, and none of them are necessarily right or wrong. What matters most is that both partners are comfortable with the way the money is handled. It is important that major decisions be made together and that each partner has some money that's theirs to spend however they wish. And remember that your money managing system will need to evolve over time. Keep it flexible enough to change as your family does.

• And as your family changes, the one thing you can count on is that the cost will go up. Even if you don't buy them designer jeans and their own cars, kids are expensive. It's important that your stepfamily have a system for dealing with kids and cash, from allowances to school fees. Whether kids should get allowances, how much is appropriate, what they should be expected to pay for out of their own money, and all the other questions about kids and money need to be answered for your family. The "right" answer depends on your family circumstances, your income, the ages and number of your kids, what you believe about money, and what works in your household.

The system you use is less important than the fact that you have one and use it consistently. However, there are some elements that a stepfamily's money-for-kids system should include:

1. Be fair. Decisions about allowances, payment for chores, and who buys what all need to be based on kids' ages rather than whose kids they are. If the two parts of the family have had different arrangements about money, it's essential for the new family to develop a new system that treats all the kids fairly.

2. Work together. It's crucial for you and your spouse to be a team on this issue. Work out your own money disagreements together before you deal with the kids. Don't go behind the other's back to slip kids an extra $20.00 bill or buy something you have previously agreed the kids should pay for themselves. This teaches kids to disregard the other parent, to be irresponsible about money, and to be manipulative.

Be matter-of-fact about differences between households. If you spend time in two different families, there are bound to be differences in the way money is handled. Perhaps the best way to deal with this situation is to be matter-of-fact about acknowledging differences. "Yes, I know you get more allowance at your mother's house, but this is the way we do things here." You don't have to defend your practices as the best; you don't have to attack the other household. You certainly don't have to allow yourself to be manipulated into outdoing the other parent. If you are comfortable that your method is fair, and if you don't respond in panic to every hint that the other parent does it better, kids will soon learn that they can't con you. And they can be flexible enough to accept the differences between households.

4. Accept the fact that you can't control money that former spouses spend or don't spend on the kids. Maybe your ex is just barely getting by and hardly manages to pay child support, while your spouse's ex is financially successful and routinely takes your stepkids on extravagant vacations or buys them expensive gifts. This is bound to cause some jealousy and resentment among your kids. Yet it wouldn't be fair to your stepkids to try to deny them the opportunities their other parent can give them. Getting overly involved in a situation like this will only make it more difficult. Your best choice is to be as fair as you can within your own household and not to worry about what the other parents do.

Planning and Communication

For a couple newly in love, caught up in romance and rosy expectations, money is a difficult issue to bring up. It may feel untrusting or crass to ask questions like, "How do you feel about helping to support my kids?" or, "What do we do about our separate debts?" or, "What about our wills?"

Tough as they may be, those questions are critical ones. Money issues are instrumental in breaking up many second marriages. Talking about money ahead of time and along the way is vital.

One of the areas that deserves particular attention is long-term financial planning. This can get complicated in second families. If young children are to be provided for through life insurance, should the beneficiary be the former spouse, the new spouse, or the kids themselves? Do you as a couple pay for kids' college educations, or should they assume that responsibility themselves? Maybe a former spouse is legally entitled to benefits from a pension plan. Maybe adult children feel a second spouse shouldn't share in their parents' assets. The right answer to any of these questions, of course, depends on your particular family circumstances. But you can't find those answers without talking about the questions.

Discussing money isn't easy, because there are usually so many emotions tangled up in the finances. This is even more of a problem in a stepfamily. In our family, for example, I have always felt guilty about spending money on my kids, because Dean has always earned most of the money and because I have received almost no child support from Gary. This is in spite of the fact that Dean has assured me from the first that my contribution in being the primary parent at home is extremely valuable to him. Those feelings are my own "stuff" about money, and they don't necessarily have a lot to do with the cold, hard facts of our family's finances.

Another former stepfamily I know broke up over money problems. The primary issue wasn't the lack of money, but the couple's feelings and beliefs about it. She had previously been married to a man who earned a great deal of money, had resented having to support herself as a single parent, and felt she should be entitled to stay home with her kids and be supported by her second husband. He, who had no kids and was appalled at how much they cost, didn't feel it was his obligation to support someone else's children. The couple weren't able to reconcile these conflicting core beliefs.

It's important for discussions about money or financial planning to include both partner's feelings as well as the dollar amounts and bottom lines. And if you can, please talk about money before resentments build up and make it even more difficult. All too often, financial discussions start when one partner's resentment finally explodes and the shouting starts. That can be constructive in the long run, but it certainly isn't much fun.

If there are unresolved money issues that are causing tension in your stepfamily, and you 'd like to start discussing them before you get to the shouting, how might you get started? First, some ways *not* to do it.

1. Don't invite your spouse out to lunch or dinner with the unspoken goal of talking about money. If they're expecting a pleasant date, they'll feel blindsided when you bring up difficult issues. It's fine to plan a meeting for this purpose, but make your intention clear ahead of time.

2. Don't attack your spouse. "You never want my kids to have anything!" isn't the most productive way to open a discussion.

3. Leave the kids out of it. Even if the topic is allowances or how much to pay for prom, discuss it with your partner first and then involve the kids as appropriate. Otherwise you're sending an open invitation for kids to manipulate you both.

Instead, try some of these strategies to get started talking about this tough issue:

1. Almost all couples talk about money occasionally—when doing the taxes, when considering a major purchase, when paying bills, when one of them gets a raise or a different job, when the roof starts leaking. Take advantage of these times to push the conversation further and open up issues you feel a need to discuss.

This works best if you start by matching your partner's mood rather than jumping in at random. If your spouse is yelling about how much it's going to cost to fix the car, you don't get far by saying, "Well, I'm sick and tired of paying for the whole family every time we go someplace." A more useful beginning would be something like, "I'm upset about that, too. Maybe we need some kind of monthly budget that's flexible enough to cover unexpected expenses and maybe entertainment costs."

2. Use a magazine article or a book on budgeting or investing as a way of starting to talk about money. It might be easiest to start with more neutral topics first and gradually work up to the ones which are more significant for your family.

3. If your own separate finances justify it, make an appointment with an accountant or financial planner. Invite your

142

partner to come along. This is neutral ground that can make it more comfortable to start a discussion.

4. Don't feel that you have to hash out every single money issue in your family all at once. Start gradually. Talk about one small issue, like whether to increase kids' allowances or how much to budget for groceries, when it comes up. Practicing on the smaller things will make it easier to start discussing the bigger issues.

Eleven

Who Moved The Bottom Line?

Whether you're negotiating in a corporate boardroom or at the kitchen table, it's important to know where your bottom line is. All good parents have principles and positions with their children which are too important for compromise. Kids learn to respect and honor the bottom-line positions and understand that, in this family, some behavior simply is not acceptable.

The reason those bottom lines are effective, of course, is that they are backed up by the usually unspoken but clearly understood ultimatum: "I am the parent here, and I am in charge. If you don't like it, that's too bad." When kids rebel, the bottom line is a safety net which keeps them from pushing the boundaries too far. Even when there is conflict, everybody understands that the parents are ultimately in charge.

In a blended family, that bottom line can lose some of its power. It's vulnerable to being undermined by other parents or stepparents. If there's conflict in one household, kids can always threaten: "I'll go live with Mom or Dad." If divorced parents back each other up and don't allow kids to manipulate them, this threat is an empty one. But if parents work against each other, the kids have an effective weapon—one which ultimately, of course, hurts themselves more than anyone if they are allowed to use it. This is one of the things that can make divorce damaging to kids and can make stepfamilying so tough.

You Couldn't Live Together, but Maybe You Can Work Together

Manipulation is a tried-and-true technique for getting what you want from other people. Most kids are past masters at it by the time they are four. If they are lucky, their parents won't let them win at it very often. When parents are divorced, they are vulnerable because of their own pain and their guilt over what the divorce might be doing to the kids, so the stakes go up in the manipulation game. Ideally, that vulnerability doesn't last long, and parents regain control. When a parent remarries, though, opportunity opens up again and the manipulation game is dragged out of the closet and dusted off.

It's probably safe to say that all kids will try some manipulation of parents and stepparents in the early days of a stepfamily, whether they are trying to hang onto a position of power, to get rid of a stepparent, or to do whatever else they can to cope with the latest upheaval in their lives. This doesn't mean the kids are doing anything wrong—they're just using the tools they have in order to get what they think they need. But parents are doing something wrong if they let themselves be manipulated. Kids need the security of knowing that they aren't in charge, that they don't make the decisions in the family, and that there is a limit beyond which they cannot go.

If kids in your family are trying to pit one household or parent against the other, the most effective response is for parents to present a united front. If divorced parents aren't still out to get one another and are mature enough to put the kids' best interests first, this isn't that hard.

The first time Dean's kids came to live with us, when Stephanie was ten, she would sneak out of bed after she thought we were asleep and make plaintive phone calls to her mother. She hated it at our house, I didn't like her, Dean and I were mean to her, she was going to get sick if she had to stay there, please couldn't Jeri just come get her. Those phone calls were terribly difficult for all of us. Jeri's first instinct, of course, like any parent's, was to rescue her child. She didn't really believe Stephanie's allegations, but she didn't want to just dismiss them, either. For a while she took the calls, trying to be supportive. But the support only encouraged Stephanie to crank up the heat. She was spending most of her energy trying to get moved back to her mother's instead of using it to learn how to get comfortable at our house.

After a week or so, Jeri talked to us about the situation. When she had reassured herself that we weren't really doing anything awful to Stephanie, she stopped playing the game. She essentially started telling Stephanie over and over, "This is the way things are. You are living at your dad's house, and you need to work things out over there." Because she backed us up, Dean and I were able to get on with the job of building a stepfamily at our house.

If a former spouse isn't cooperative, though, a situation like this can do a lot of damage. If this kind of manipulation is going on at your house, and it seems to be working, it's important to try to end it if you can. The first step is for you or your spouse to talk with the other parent. Even if you don't expect a positive response, ask anyway if you possibly can. If you approach the situation from the perspective of "what is best for this child that we both love," instead of blaming or attacking, you just might get some cooperation. If you don't, at least you have made an attempt.

If a former spouse simply won't work with you to stop a child's manipulation, there isn't a great deal you can do. It is essential that you and your spouse work as a team and not let the manipulating grow until it divides you. You can be as pleasant and matter-of-fact as possible about differences between households. You can do your best to make children comfortable in your household without turning it upside down in order to placate them. And you can be patient. If the manipulation game doesn't "get" you and your spouse, perhaps eventually everyone will get tired of it and stop playing.

146

Relax and Be Yourself

You don't make chili or pancakes the right way. You're too fussy about loud radios. Your don't wear cool clothes like Mom or Dad does. There's too much onion in your meatloaf. You don't take the family out to eat enough. You buy birthday cakes instead of baking them. You make kids go to bed too early or do too many chores or use the wrong kind of shampoo.

In short, you aren't just like your stepkids' mother or father. (If you were, of course, your spouse probably wouldn't have married you.) Your household isn't going to be just like the other ones your kids or stepkids live in. And the kids will be quick to let you know about all the things you don't do right. For a while I heard, "Mom doesn't make Peter do that," or "Mom thinks we don't need to do this," until I was ready to scream.

The best answer to criticisms like this is, "Oh?" Don't get into explanations or justifications. Don't let the kids con you into thinking everything you do is wrong. If you want to change the way you make chili to accommodate your stepkids' tastes, that's great. But don't play the game of comparing yourself to their other parent. It's a game you can only lose, especially when you realize that what you're comparing yourself to is an exaggerated and distorted image. You aren't a perfect parent or stepparent. Neither is anyone else, despite what your stepkids may tell you.

Besides, a kid's definition of a "perfect parent" probably isn't even going to be a valid one. They might think you should let them stay up all night, go out six times a week, or eat junk food three times a day. But you can't base your parenting on what you think the kids will like; you have to base it on what you think they need. If you are doing your job as a parent at all well, the kids aren't going to like you all the time. Remember that this isn't a game where the parent or stepparent with the highest approval rating wins.

You have your own ways of parenting, your own ways of managing a household, your own ideas and attitudes about what's important. You certainly need to be flexible and adjust some of those styles as you work to make everyone comfortable in your stepfamily. But you don't need to try to make yourself over into something you're not. Don't set yourself up for failure and guilt by trying to be a homemade-bread kind of parent if your style is McDonald's instead. One of the secrets of good parenting and stepparenting is to be the kind of good parent you can comfortably be.

A lot of the time the differences between households are more style than substance. The kids can adjust to this; they do it all the time. Maybe their second grade teacher insisted on a quiet classroom with all the desks in rows, while their third grade teacher let them study in groups or move around freely. Maybe their algebra teacher lets them chew gum while their science teacher doesn't. They accommodate themselves to such differences perfectly well. In the same way, they can adjust to the fact that the style is different at your house than it is at their other parent's. If you are matter-of-fact instead of defensive about the differences, the kids will learn to be, as well.

Stand Firm On the Big Stuff

Stephanie was a sophomore in high school when she decided she wanted to stay at her mother's house instead of moving back in with us for the winter. When Jeri called Dean to tell him that Stephanie wanted to stay there, she added, "And I've told her I won't make her go."

As a mother, I can empathize with that response. If Rachel were living with her dad part of the time, and she told me she wanted to stay with me, I certainly wouldn't have any desire to tell her, "No, you have to go." What was upsetting for Dean and me was primarily the fact that the decision was made so completely before we even knew anything was going on. We weren't given the courtesy of a discussion with Jeri first. Because Stephanie already knew she had her mother's complete support, we had no negotiating position left to persuade either of them that Stephanie should continue to live part of the time with us. We probably wouldn't have negotiated too hard, anyway—the prospect of living with a teenager who absolutely doesn't want to be in your house isn't exactly a delightful one. But because the bottom line was jerked right out from under us, we had no chance to even be a part of any discussion.

As all the kids have grown older, I'm beginning to realize that the specialty of the teenage years is feeling misunderstood. Most of them would like to think they were adopted, because they surely couldn't have been born to these horribly ordinary parents who can't possibly relate to them. Some of their friends have cool parents, who seem to be more sympathetic, more flexible, and much more fun. They wouldn't mind moving out of their own oppressive households if they could live with someone like that. Instead, they are forced to commit unnatural acts such as cleaning their rooms and sitting at the dinner table with the rest of the family.

Though my kids would find it hard to believe, I do remember that "nobody understands me" feeling. I was never an active rebel as a teenager; I didn't have horrible fights with my parents or shout and slam doors. Instead, I remember hiding in my room and writing some really bad poetry (which thankfully has not survived) about how unique I was. But I never once thought about moving out. This was mostly because, underneath the sighing and self-centeredness, I really loved my parents and didn't want to leave. It also may have been because the possibility simply never entered my mind. It just wasn't one of the available choices.

For kids in a stepfamily, unfortunately, moving out usually is one of the possible choices. Parents have lost the unspoken bottom line of "Because I'm the parent, and that's the way it is."

149

There may be times when it's best for a child to live in one parent's home rather than the other's. There are situations when stepparents are genuinely unfair, immature, unloving, or abusive. There also families where none of the adults, parents or stepparents, spouses or former spouses, are able to do a good job. No child should have to grow up in that kind of a family, and it would be a blessing if they had a chance to live somewhere else and get better parenting.

But there are also families where parents and stepparents on both sides are doing just fine. Maybe one set of parents is stricter than the other. Maybe one household has more money, or more cars, or plays more, or takes the kids camping more. But both of them have something unique to offer. In a situation like this, no child should have the handicap of knowing that, any time things get a little tough, they can just leave.

When teenage conflicts, complicated by stepfamily struggles, result in a child's leaving home, everybody loses. One household tends to be labeled as the "bad family," which can cause hard feelings and misperceptions on both sides. The child and the parents who have the difficulty don't get a chance to work things out, so the conflict gets covered up instead of resolved. The kid learns that the way to deal with a problem is to avoid it and go somewhere else that looks easier. And the unique qualities that one family can provide to the child don't get passed on.

Children—even when they are teenagers who know everything—don't understand that what they *want* might be the exact opposite of what they *need*. What they see as unreasonable rigidity might very well be good parenting with appropriate limits and boundaries. For that reason, kids aren't the ones who should decide what is the best place for them to live. Ideally, those decisions ought to be made by parents, working together, whose primary concern is the ultimate well-being of the child. Unfortunately, parents who are struggling with their own stuff don't always make decisions in such a mature way. (If all of us were able to be that well-balanced, we probably would never have been divorced in the first place.)

The reason all of this is so damaging is because parents, faced with the insecurity of no solid bottom line, tend to abandon their principles. In a traditional family, if the 12-year-old defiantly refuses to do homework or the 14-year-old wants to stay out till midnight on school nights or the 16-year-old skips school, parents have the upper hand. They can stay in there and fight it out, knowing that the kids might hate them passionately for a while, but that ultimately their authority will prevail—most often to the relief of the kids, who don't even really want complete freedom. But if parents know the kid has the ultimate weapon of, "Then I'll go live with Mom or Dad and never come back here," they are too often tempted to wimp out. The results are kids with too few limits, a parent with less self-respect, and a cycle of destructive irresponsibility.

The only answer to this problem, as far as I know, is for parents and stepparents without a bottom line to act as if they still have one. Even if kids are holding, "I'll move out," over your head, it's essential that you stick to your principles on the big stuff. Yes, you need to be flexible and understanding to live comfortably in a stepfamily. No, that absolutely doesn't mean compromising your standards or your values. If skipping school, smoking, using drugs, being disrespectful, or flunking classes are unacceptable behavior at your house, you can't back down just because a child threatens to leave.

On an issue like this, you might "lose' in the short term. Because if a child chooses to move out, and if their other parent doesn't back you up, there simply isn't a lot you can do. In extreme cases, you might be able to go to court to enforce keeping a child in your house, but many situations aren't blatant enough to justify such a move. Instead, your best choice might be to maintain your position, keep channels of communication open as best you can, and think long-term. In the long run, it's more valuable for the child to see you hold to your standards than for them to stay with you because you compromised.

If you abandon your principles on important issues, you are selling yourself out. You are saying that you will give up your self-respect just so a teenager won't be mad at you. That's exactly the wrong thing to teach your children. Instead, for your kids as well as yourself, you need to hold onto your integrity as a person and as a parent.

Twelve

Heartaches and Heartbreaks

I am writing this on the Monday after a tough weekend. Amy and Peter just moved out again. It was time for their annual spring relocation to their mother's house. They packed their stuff with excitement, pleased to be going back to Mom's. She was delighted to have them back. Dean, who takes a long-term view of things, told them goodbye cheerfully. Rachel was sorry to lose their companionship but glad to have the downstairs bathroom and the telephone all to herself. And I cried.

I have greatly enjoyed the past six months with the three younger kids all here. I'll miss the daily presence of Amy and Peter, even though they will be here every other weekend. But the pain I feel over their moving isn't for the fact that they're leaving—it's over the fact that they are so happy to go. No matter how long all of us have been part of the same family, how close we have become, or how well we usually get along by now, our house is always second best. Mom's house is their first home. My saner adult self tells me that's just the way things are, and it's okay. My critical self tells me it's because I haven't tried hard enough. And my little-kid self just feels hurt about it.

Going back to Pollyanna, I actually can find something to be glad about in this situation. At least I feel bad about their moving out instead of being delighted to see them go. It would be awful to live half of every year with stepkids if we were in constant conflict and mutually couldn't wait for the six months to be over.

I have preached all the way through this book that you should choose to love your stepkids. I honestly and deeply believe you should. What you will gain from that choice is beyond measure. But deciding to make the effort to be loving doesn't mean you will automatically be sprinkled with sparkling fairy dust and rewarded with a life that's free from hurts. Quite the contrary. When you choose to love, you make yourself vulnerable to the hurts that go with caring about anyone else. If you love your stepkids, you will always come second and you will always have to share their love with other parents who come first. Choosing to love your spouse and your stepkids may mean you will lose, at least temporarily, some closeness you have established with your own kids. And loving people who don't necessarily love or even like each other can open you up to all kinds of pain.

Among the realities of stepfamilying are the heartaches. Some families have more and some have less, but every family will have its share. You can let them defeat you, retreating into bitterness or simply leaving. Or you can choose to learn and grow from them, letting them help you become more mature and more compassionate.

Walking Through the Dark Valleys

The worst time for me so far in our eight years of stepfamilying was when Loren, as a sophomore in high school, had a fight with his stepdad and abruptly moved from our house to his dad's. I was angry at Loren for his part in provoking the situation, I was angry at Dean because he didn't handle it as well as he could have, and I was especially angry at Gary because his reaction escalated the conflict instead of doing anything to resolve it. Loren felt he had been mistreated and expected that I would immediately throw Dean out of the house. When I didn't, he accused me bitterly of choosing his stepfather instead of him—which essentially was what I did. For the next two years I had hardly any contact with Loren, and although there has been considerable healing since, the pain of that break still affects our relationship.

154

Unfortunately, painful situations like this happen all too often in stepfamilies. But they don't have to destroy your family. All of you can get through them, recover from them, and learn from them. Getting through the heartbreaks is never easy, but there are a few things you can do to make it a little less difficult.

1. Get help and support. Don't pretend everything is just fine when it isn't. When you admit you're having a tough time, you can get the help you need. As I keep saying, find a safe place to talk about your hurts and begin to resolve them. You can do this in a support group, with friends, through a church, or with members of your family. For the serious issues, you might need professional help as well. Please don't be afraid or embarrassed to use resources that can make a big difference.

2. Remember "this, too, shall pass." Yes, this hurts now. Yes, it feels awful to be attacked or betrayed or otherwise injured. But it won't last forever. Kids grow up, adults learn new ways of reacting, situations change, and stepfamilies mature. Remember that time is healing.

3. Take one day at a time. You don't have to experience or handle all the heartache at once. For today, concentrate on getting through one day of grief or anger or hurt. Don't load yesterday's and tomorrow's on top of it. Yesterday's pain is gone, and tomorrow will be time enough to worry about tomorrow's.

4. Make other members of your stepfamily your allies, not your enemies. Let them know you hurt in ways that ask for their support instead of attacking them. If you are struggling with one of your stepchildren, don't take your anger or hurt out on the rest of them. If you are angry at your former spouse, don't pressure your kids to take sides. Don't pretend within the family that nothing is going on—it can be helpful for everybody to talk about it whatever is happening. But don't use the family as a place to vent your feelings. Do your screaming and gnashing of teeth somewhere else.

5. Do change the things you can. Part of the pain I had—and still have—over the break with Loren resulted from guilt over my

own failure to try harder to keep in touch with him. Gary at that time refused to give me his phone number, so I couldn't talk to Loren. But I could have written him letters or sent messages with Rachel to let him know how much I cared about him. Had I done what I could do, it would have been easier to accept the part that I couldn't change.

It's Nothing Personal

Last week a young man we know, who is just a year older than Loren, was seriously injured in an accident. This morning's newspaper in our small city included two obituaries of newborn babies. As I was working on this chapter, I received a phone call from my mother telling me that a family friend had died of cancer.

It would be incredibly self-centered to think that being part of a stepfamily gives any of us a monopoly on heartaches. Life is filled with challenges and hurts. Some of them result from choices people make, while others seem to happen at random. Because you have chosen to become part of a stepfamily, you've increased your chances of having the particular hurts which go along with that choice. But not every bit of pain in your life from here on is going to be the result of being in a stepfamily.

Nor is every bit of grief that does come from being in a stepfamily going to be the result of something you did. For one thing, you certainly don't do all of the parenting for all of the kids in your family. For another, you don't cause and can't control the actions of other family members. Your spouse, your kids, your stepkids, and everybody's former spouses will all make their own choices. Some of those choices will cause you pain. Sometimes the pain might be deliberately inflicted. More often, though, it will grow out of someone else's hurt or thoughtlessness, and you won't be its direct target.

So when building a successful stepfamily seems to be just too much of a struggle, remember that there's nothing personal here.

Stepfamilying is just the particular form that your life's challenges happen to be taking at the moment. God is not out to get you just because you have some struggles. Life is difficult, not because you're part of a stepfamily, but because life is difficult. Once you accept the fact that it is difficult, you stop wasting energy protesting, "This isn't fair!" And then life becomes less difficult. (If this doesn't make sense to you, please go get yourself a copy of M. Scott Peck's *The Road Less Traveled*, which is one of the most valuable books I have ever read.)

Bitterness Corrodes the Vessel

We've already discussed in Chapter Seven the importance of letting go. Anger and pain, held onto and nursed, turn into nasty resentments that are extremely destructive. It's a bit like leaving leftovers in the refrigerator for weeks, until they turn into something green and poisonous and really ugly. If you carry resentment, it grows into a poison which is more toxic to you than to anyone else. It eventually spills over and affects the people around you, but the most damage is to your own emotional health. For your own sake, you need to let resentments go.

Just imagine for a moment that you are required to carry a bag with you all through your life. Every time someone hurts you or offends you or makes you angry, you put a resentment into the bag. It won't take long until that bag is huge and so heavy that you can't lift it and you're forced to drag it along behind. You can't put it down, and it makes everything you do much more difficult. Eventually you will stop even trying to run, to jump, or to dance. Just plodding slowly along will be all you can manage.

If you choose not to keep resentments every time something upsets you, but you toss them all into the trash instead as you go along, your bag won't ever get full. You can carry it lightly in one hand, drape it comfortably over your shoulder, or tuck it into your belt. It won't ever be big and bulky enough to get in your way.

157

When you carry around resentments, the emotional burden of them holds you back, weighs you down, and keeps you from doing what you want to do. It makes perfect sense that you ought to let go of them instead. But just because it makes perfect sense doesn't mean it's easy to do. I wish I could tell you how to go about it. This is something I'm not very good at yet.

With practice, I'm getting better at not letting small hurts grow into resentments. One thing that's been helpful for me is to make a point of acknowledging and expressing it when I get angry. I absolutely hate conflict, so I tend to keep my mouth shut and try to avoid it. Sometimes this works, but sometimes it just leaves my anger shut up inside to fester. It's important for me to dig up enough courage to say something to the person I'm angry with, even if it scares me to do so. Then we can deal with the issue and move on.

There are times, of course, when confronting the other person isn't appropriate for one reason or another. Maybe you're angry at a former spouse, but you know expressing your anger is just going to make a bad situation worse. Maybe you're unreasonably angry at a stepchild, and saying so wouldn't accomplish anything except damaging the bonds you're starting to form. In these cases, it's still important to acknowledge to yourself that you're angry. You can talk to a friend, write something in a journal, or just stomp around privately and mutter for a while. Do this with the intention of getting the anger out of your system, rather than feeding it and helping it grow.

Twelve-step programs recommend taking a continuous personal inventory and promptly admitting it when you are wrong. Many people do this on a daily basis, often doing a quick mental review at bedtime to see if there is anything they need to take care of. It can be useful to do this with resentments as well as with wrongs you may have done to others. Am I angry about this? Am I uncomfortable because of that? Is this incident something I need to deal with, or can I forget about it? It's useful for me to think of this as a sort of mental straightening-up at the end of the day.

When you get ready for bed, you brush your teeth and hang up your clothes and put your dirty socks in the hamper so everything is tidy. You can do the same with any resentments you've picked up that day, shaking them out and putting them in the trash so they aren't cluttering up the place.

These strategies are useful for letting go of resentment over small hurts. I still haven't figured out what to do about the big ones. I do know that it's important to accept and acknowledge your losses and pain, to talk about them and get support, and to allow yourself time to grieve over them. It's also essential for your well-being that you eventually let them go instead of allowing them to embitter you. Pain and loss can drive wedges between people. Don't make your stepfamilying harder by letting that happen. Life is simply too short to waste by holding onto resentments and grudges which make yourself and other family members miserable. Instead, do your best to let losses soften you, increase your capacity for compassion and empathy, and allow you to grow closer to the others in your family.

Forgive and Forget

Writing this book has meant taking a look back at the past eight years. Some of the memories have been funny, some have been heartwarming, some have made me squirm with embarrassment, and some have been painful. I have been reminded too vividly of all the mistakes I have made and continue to make.

As a result, I am beginning to feel like an enormous fraud. I've been writing so earnestly about the importance of communication, choosing to love your stepchildren, being flexible, being compassionate, and being an adult. I truly do mean and believe all those things. But some days I don't manage to do any of them. It seems to me right now that if my children and stepchildren read this book, they will either laugh out loud or get

159

terribly angry at my presumption in trying to tell other stepparents how to do something which I am so far short of mastering myself.

Part of me knows that this feeling is temporary, that I am letting myself be discouraged at the moment because I've been wallowing in "should have known better." I do know that is the truth. It is also the truth that I have been and continue to be far from a perfect mother and stepmother. I am too often impatient, too often critical, too often rigid, and too seldom fun. I hug the kids too little and bark at them too much. I lecture too often and listen too seldom.

And, as my husband would say, "So?" What kind of a standard am I measuring myself against? How many perfect parents or stepparents do I know? He isn't one. Neither is his ex-wife. Neither is my ex-husband. I don't know anyone who is, actually. And when I stop to think about it, the kids aren't so darned flawless, either.

All of us are human. All of us mess up. All parents, no matter how loving they are or how hard they try, make mistakes. A stepfamily especially gives you ample opportunities for mistakes, because it has so many more moving parts. So you might as well resign yourself to the fact that, as a stepparent, you aren't always going to do it right. (While you're at it, you might as well also get used to the idea that various kids, stepkids, and former spouses will be happy to point out any mistakes you might not have noticed yourself.)

And of course, you aren't the only one in your stepfamily who makes mistakes. All of you will have fights and misunderstandings, disagreements and struggles. You will all hurt each other, intentionally and otherwise. Those hurts can destroy your stepfamily. Or they can be a step along the way to getting to know each other better. One of the critical factors that determines which they will be is forgiveness.

Forgiveness has two faces. The first one is forgiving yourself for past mistakes; the other is forgiving others for things they have done which hurt you. Neither one is particularly easy, but they are

160

equally important in moving beyond hurts and getting on with your life.

The first step in forgiving yourself is to accept the fact that you have made mistakes in your stepparenting. It isn't useful to spend years writhing in shame over those mistakes, to beat yourself up for them, or to let other people run over you because you feel so guilty over them. Instead, you need to forgive yourself and move on.

Forgiving yourself is not the same as making excuses or pretending nothing happened. For example: Last fall, when we decided our second-hand table and chairs were ready for the Salvation Army, I bought a dining room set. I'm still wondering why, out of all the salespeople at all the furniture stores in town, I wound up dealing with Frances. I think it must have been a sin I committed in some previous life. First Frances ordered the wrong table. Then she found the table I wanted in the store, but it was broken. When she reordered, she ordered the wrong table again. Then the warehouse was out of the right table. The chairs that came with the first table were the wrong ones. The chairs that came with the second table were damaged. After ten or twelve weeks of this, I finally went to the sales manager, got my money back, and went to a different furniture store to get a table. The sales manager had Frances call to apologize for all the hassle. Her apology was essentially, "I'm sorry you thought there was a problem." She blamed the store management, the manufacturer, and the delivery system, conveniently forgetting that she was the one who ordered the wrong table twice. She finished with, "Well, I guess I'm just too human."

This is not what it means to forgive yourself for your mistakes. It doesn't mean lightly saying "oops" and imagining that's enough to make everything okay. Before you can forgive yourself, you have to acknowledge that damage was done and take responsibility for whatever you did wrong. Then you have to do what you can to make amends or fix the problem.

Making amends goes beyond simply apologizing. It may start with saying you're sorry, but the heart of it is changing what you do. If your behavior has hurt someone in the past, the best way to make amends is to behave differently in the future. Once you have begun to change your behavior so you don't make the same mistake again, then you're ready to forgive yourself. Self-forgiveness essentially means to stop beating yourself up for being less than perfect and to get on with your life.

Forgiving someone else is somewhat the same process. Again, you can't just say, "Oh, that's okay," and pretend nothing happened. There's a difference between forgiveness and denial—or forgiveness and being afraid to deal with something. You have to acknowledge to yourself that a wrong was done, even if the other person doesn't make the same acknowledgment. You can't pardon someone if you're pretending no offense was ever committed.

Forgiving doesn't mean allowing someone to hurt you over again in the same ways, either. You don't have to accept abuse or put yourself back in a position where you will be hurt. If the other person has not accepted responsibility or changed their behavior, you can change yours in order to protect yourself. Forgiveness isn't the same as stupidity. (I've long since forgiven Frances for her table-ordering errors—because of the entertainment value of the whole story, if nothing else. But that doesn't mean I'm ever going to buy any more furniture from her.)

It's important not to see forgiveness as a "one-up/one-down" situation where you graciously pardon someone because you are better than they are. That kind of forgiveness is destructive because it keeps people apart by labeling the forgiver as the good guy and the forgivee as the bad guy. Genuine forgiveness, on the other hand, is a realistic acceptance of someone else as human and flawed, just like you are. It increases understanding instead of keeping distance between you. This is one reason that it's so important.

It's easy to think of forgiveness as something high-minded and saintly, a little bit Biblical and somewhat above us ordinary mortals. It really isn't that at all. It's actually quite practical and logical. It's very much the same as letting go of resentment—a way of tossing out the emotional garbage as you go so it doesn't keep getting in your way.

It isn't realistic to think you and the other members of your stepfamily aren't going to hurt each other. You will sometimes be impatient or unreasonable, you and your spouse will disagree, the kids will do things that are silly or mean or just plain dumb. It doesn't help the family to beat yourself up endlessly over past mistakes or to keep reminding other people of theirs. All of you have been doing the best you can. When you let go of the past by forgiving each other, you can focus your energy on doing even better in the present and the future.

Thirteen

Will the Real Adult
Please Stand Up?

Some blended families thrive and grow happily together. Some hang in there, struggling but managing to survive. And some come painfully apart. What makes the difference?

It's not easy to isolate why one stepfamily works and another doesn't. But there are some factors which many successful stepfamilies share. They learn to communicate and solve problems. They are flexible. They are committed to each other. They have realistic expectations. The most important thing successful blended families have in common, however, can be summed up like this:

The single most important factor in the success or failure of a blended family is the emotional health of the adults in it.

If that doesn't make sense to you, check out the following example:

Suppose Adam is an alcoholic. He's not the skid-row bum type; he's a successful salesman who has never missed a day of work because of his drinking. But he drinks after work with his co-workers or customers; he buys beer by the case; and on weekends he's passed out on the couch by suppertime. He doesn't have much interaction with his two daughters except to yell at them to be quiet when he has a hangover—though he gets emotional over his beer when he's telling his bar buddies how much he loves his kids.

After twelve years or so of this, Adam's wife divorces him. He keeps on drinking, nursing a mighty resentment over the way she has treated him and taken away his kids. After a couple years he meets Toni in his favorite bar. Newly divorced herself, she consoles him over the terrible things his ex-wife has done. They marry six weeks later, and he moves in with Toni and her three kids. He's still doing okay at his job, still missing his first family, and still drinking. How well do you think he and Toni will be able to cope with the stress and complications of a stepfamily?

But what if instead the second part of the story goes like this: Shocked by the divorce, Adam goes to treatment for his alcoholism. He becomes actively involved in Alcoholics Anonymous and builds up a support system of recovering friends. He goes to therapy to deal with his pain over the divorce and with the issues underlying his drinking. He starts to build relationships with his children. After a couple of years, he meets Toni through a mutual AA friend. They date for almost a year, getting to know each other and each other's kids, working out conflicts that come up, and building a commitment to each other. Then they marry. This time how well do you think they will be able to cope with the stress and complications of a stepfamily?

Most stepfamilies are created by partners who have been divorced. Something causes those divorces. Sometimes people do simply grow apart, or they may have conflicting goals and desires about having children or making career and lifestyle choices. More commonly, though, people divorce because of such issues as chemical addiction, emotional or physical abuse, an inability to resolve problems, or one partner's excessive dependency on the other.

Those issues aren't magically cured by getting divorced. They need to be healed by an active effort to learn new beliefs and patterns of behavior. Such change is made easier with the help of therapy and support groups. People who don't do such healing, but who go into a second marriage without addressing the issues that caused the first marriage to end, are setting themselves up for failure.

Addicts who are still using won't be able to put their second family ahead of their drugs any more than they did the first family. A man who has never gotten to know his children because of his workaholism isn't going to be able to build a relationship with his stepchildren, either. A woman who has always let herself be abused because she doesn't value herself is just as likely to marry an abusive husband the second time as the first.

A stepfamily is harder to live in than a traditional family. There are more built-in tensions, more moving parts, and more potential for conflict. It's absurd to expect someone who couldn't make it in a traditional family to be successful in a stepfamily, unless in the meantime they have changed.

If your blended family is having serious difficulties, maybe the place to look for solutions isn't the stepfamily itself. Maybe the problems go back further. Some possibilities might include these: Is anyone in the family an addict? (Keep in mind that addictions involve more than drugs or alcohol—people can be addicted to substances or behaviors such as food, work, gambling, sex, shopping, television, or computer games.) Is there a serious inability to communicate about important issues? Have children been placed in inappropriate adult roles? Is there a lot of anger that seems out of proportion to the events that trigger it?

Though they certainly can make it harder to build a functional stepfamily, problems like these aren't stepfamily issues. They are personal issues. Until they are healed, it will be extremely hard to build a healthy family or stepfamily. If some of these problems are affecting your well-being and that of your family, please do whatever you can to take care of them.

Act Your Age

I am an adult. I have proof—it says so in purple capital letters on my season pass at the ski area. Besides, I know about things like income tax returns and retirement plans and using the plunger when the bathroom stool overflows. When I look in the mirror, I see some gray hairs and lines around my eyes that imply a certain level of maturity.

Those gray hairs aren't the entire truth, though. No matter how much I may know, how mature I may look, or even how mature I am capable of acting, there is still part of me that feels like a child in certain situations. Unfortunately for good stepparenting, many of those situations involve my stepkids.

Trying to be a mature, capable adult in a stepfamily when you often feel like a vulnerable child is an enormous challenge. You can't comfortably let your spouse have some time with his or her children when you're afraid they will push you out of the family. You can't be a strong and mature stepparent to a self-centered teenager when you feel about eight years old and your feelings are hurt by every rude or careless remark. You can't win a power struggle with a stepchild when you perceive that child as older and more powerful than you are.

If you often feel hurt by your stepkids' words or actions, if you are jealous of them, or if you usually see your stepchildren as being more powerful than you are, perhaps the root of the problem is in your own childhood. All of us have an inner child-self that is sensitive and vulnerable. This is the part of you which gets jealous of your stepkids, has hurt feelings over little things, feels frightened in new situations, and can be incredibly petty. It's also the part of you which—when you learn to pay attention to it—intuitively knows what is right for you. This child-self is not a weakness, a sign of immaturity, or a problem. It is simply one way of describing the intuitive, sensitive, spiritual aspect of ourselves.

Left stranded in unresolved hurts or shame from childhood, that child-self can cause you to be fearful, over-sensitive, petty, and self-pitying. Taken care of and acknowledged as an inherent part of you, the child-self can be a source of power and strength. The whole issue of strengthening your inner child is too complex to go into here, but it is an important part of learning to be comfortable in the world as an adult. There are several excellent books on the subject, one of which is *Healing the Child Within*, by Dr. Charles L. Whitfield.

Being an effective stepparent is tough even if you are mature, self-confident, and emotionally healthy. It's much more difficult if your child-self is still fearful and overly vulnerable because of unhealed childhood hurts. It's hard to handle the challenges of stepparenting like an adult when you don't feel like one inside.

The irony here is that, on one hand, your stepkids will show you no mercy because to them you are a strong and capable adult. They accept the outer truth of your gray hairs and mature appearance. On the other hand, they intuitively will know your vulnerable points and will take full advantage of them. If you are afraid you don't really deserve your place in the stepfamily, or if you see the kids as more powerful than you are, they will be quick to exploit your weaknesses. (By the way, that doesn't mean that your stepkids are horrible little monsters; they are just acting like normal human beings in a situation that is hard for them, too.)

In order to improve your situation, obviously you need to get to a point where—at least most of the time—you feel like an adult inside as well as look like one outside. So how do you do that?

1. Get help. This is the kind of stuff therapy is for. Some individual counseling or a therapy group can be enormously useful in helping you make this kind of change. An ongoing support group such as Al-Anon for Adult Children or Emotions Anonymous can also be extremely valuable.

2. Acknowledge your feelings, but remember that they are separate from your actions. You don't have to throw yourself to the floor and kick and scream just because you feel about six years

old and you didn't get your own way. Sometimes just accepting that you do feel disproportionately hurt or angry can be a relief and can help keep you from acting on the feelings.

3. Fake it till you make it. Just because your knees feel like strawberry Jell-O and the butterflies in your stomach are doing the jitterbug doesn't mean you have to fall apart on the outside. Remember that most of the time you probably don't look as hurt or scared or angry as you feel. Do your best to behave the way you think an adult would act in this situation. You are more capable than you think, so pull yourself together and do your best. Then you can cry or scream or have a temper tantrum later, privately or in your support group, where your actions won't hurt yourself or anyone else in your family.

4. Always remember that your stepkids are less powerful than they seem. Regardless of their ages or their skills at manipulating or their ability to wind their parents around their little fingers, they are still kids. And they may well be even more scared and hurt inside than you are. Do your best to respond to their hurting inner children instead of to the angry or resentful image they show on the outside.

5. Let your spouse know how you feel. Try not to do this in attack mode (I just can't put up with your awful kids for one more minute!) or in guilt mode (You need to make your kids stop being so mean to me!). But an honest sharing of your vulnerability can be a good first step toward change.

6. Remember that this kind of change is your job, not anyone else's. You are responsible for the way you feel and the way you react to the other people in your stepfamily. You can't change your stepkids; you can only change the way you deal with them. The bonus here is that, when you change your attitudes and reactions, other family members will often change the way they treat you. After all, kids will only play manipulative games as long as they work. If you stop playing your half of the game, there's not much point in their continuing to play their half.

Taking Care of Yourself

When Stephanie decided that she wanted to live full-time with her mother instead of moving back in with us, Amy's first reaction was, "Does that mean I can have her room?"

Amy and Rachel had shared a bedroom at our house for six years. With not enough space, Rachel's untidiness, and Amy's talking in her sleep, the arrangement was a source of conflict. I was pleased at the idea of each girl being able to have her own room.

But when I mentioned this to a friend, she had a different view. "What about the space you need?" she asked me. "Why don't you use one of those bedrooms for an office? After all, the kids aren't the only ones with needs here. You need to take care of yourself, too."

She had a point. At that time my office was a corner of our overcrowded living room. But even though the room turned into a homework factory after school, I did have it all to myself during the day. In this particular case, Rachel and Amy needed separate bedrooms far more than I needed a separate office.

Yes, as parents and stepparents we do need to take care of ourselves. But that doesn't mean putting our needs and wants ahead of those of our kids. We are in charge of managing family resources to benefit our kids and ourselves. We shouldn't be competing with the kids for those resources.

The idea of parenting as involving sacrifice is often turned into a joke—usually involving motherhood and guilt. "After all I've done for you...!" But there's no joke about the very real fact that having children or accepting responsibility for stepchildren means inviting a great many complications into your life. You can call these complications "sacrifices" if you want; or try "delayed gratification" or "long-term thinking" or even plain old "inconvenience."

Whatever word you use, there's no getting around the fact that being a parent or stepparent quite often means putting your own wishes second. Whether it's getting up for the third time in the same night with a crying baby or rearranging schedules to take a teenager to soccer practice, parenting means doing lots of stuff we'd really just as soon not do. Stepparenting complicates the equation even more by adding in factors like the need to be flexible about holidays or to allow your new spouse time with his or her kids.

And if you aren't willing to put your own wishes second most of the time, you aren't doing your job as a parent and stepparent. Yes, good parents take care of themselves. But that doesn't mean failing to do those inconvenient but important things that the kids need. It means maintaining your sanity and energy so you're able to do them.

Taking care of yourself doesn't mean:
- Routinely ignoring your kids' and stepkids' needs because you're too tired or too sick or too busy to have energy for them.
- Leaving kids unsupervised night after night while you go out to play, to work, or to improve yourself with classes or support groups.
- Being unavailable to your kids because you're preoccupied with your own emotional needs. This is especially likely to happen after a divorce or during other stressful times. It's most damaging if it continues over a long period of time.
- Spending significant amounts of money on yourself or the house while saying no to activities or necessities for the kids. (This doesn't mean you should go around in rags while the kids wear designer jeans, either—the idea is to be fair to everybody.)

- Routinely letting kids stay up past bedtime, neglect homework, etc., to suit your convenience. (For example, being unwilling to interrupt a television program to help kids with math or take time to put them to bed.)

Taking care of yourself does mean:
- Getting enough sleep and exercise so you have the energy you need.
- Taking steps to get help if you have unhealed issues from your own childhood (abuse, parental alcoholism, etc.) that are causing problems in your adult life.
- Having a support system of friends you can talk to about problems.
- Taking occasional time away from the kids for yourself and also to nurture the relationship between you and your spouse.
- Teaching kids to pitch in and help (picking up after themselves, helping with chores, being responsible for their own homework, etc.) instead of doing everything for them.
- Setting priorities in your life so you get some of what you need without neglecting the kids. Define what is essential in your life and for your family, and put your energy into those things. Maybe taking a pottery class once a week is more essential to your well-being than vacuuming regularly. Maybe you'd rather buy your kids' clothes at rummage sales instead of the mall so you can afford to send them to gymnastics classes.

Genuinely taking care of yourself isn't being selfish or taking anything away from your family. It is doing what you need to do to be a healthy, mature adult who is capable of taking care of your kids and stepkids.

Getting Help

"Dysfunctional" was the hot buzzword a few years ago. Books on dysfunctional families topped best-seller lists. Talk shows flourished on the stories of survivors of all kinds of abuse. The concept of dysfunctional families has .been misused in some cases, with a few authors and lecturers encouraging people to settle for blaming their parents instead of working to make their own lives better. But the reason unhealthy families were pushed so strongly into our awareness is that they exist and they cause significant problems.

However, I find it helpful to remember that the word "dysfunctional" doesn't mean "sick" or "broken" or "bad." My dictionary defines dysfunction as, "in medicine, abnormal, impaired, or incomplete functioning of an organ or part." In other words, it's something that doesn't work very well.

If you grew up in a family that didn't work very well, you didn't learn how to create a family which would work. It's not too late to do that learning. If personal issues are making it harder for you to be a parent or stepparent, please do something about it. A lot of help is available, but it's up to you to make the choice to use it.

It takes a mature, emotionally stable person to be a good parent and stepparent. Perhaps you weren't that kind of person when your children were born or your stepchildren came into your life. That doesn't mean you are doomed to do a horrible job forever. You may have made mistakes in the past, but that doesn't mean you have to make the same mistakes in the future.

Remember that the most important way you teach your kids and stepkids is through the behavior you model for them. They may not listen to what you say, but they absolutely will pay attention to what you do. Working to change and grow into a healthier person is some of the best role modeling you can possibly provide. Getting help doesn't just mean taking parenting classes or learning about child development, either. If something will help you become a healthier and better person, it will help you become a better parent and stepparent.

There are tremendous resources available today for anyone who genuinely wants to change. Take advantage of them. You might start with some of these:

1. Books and tapes. It's hard to make lasting changes by relying only on your local bookstore, but the information you can find in self-help books and tapes is a valuable place to start. There are books on parenting, on stepfamilies, on dealing with anger, on healing childhood abuse, and on spiritual growth. There are as many approaches as there are authors. Keep in mind as you browse through the bookstore or library that each book or tape reflects its author's own path. You'll find various "experts" who disagree. Take what seems to apply to you, adapt it for your own particular circumstances, and let the rest go.

2. Support groups. Many communities offer parenting classes or support groups for stepfamilies. Support groups are also available for more specific situations such as chronic illnesses, bereavement, or divorce. It can be extremely helpful to get together regularly with others who are experiencing the same challenges that you are.

2. Twelve-step groups. The twelve-step program based on Alcoholics Anonymous is not just for those who have problems with drinking. It offers a way to learn to take responsibility for yourself and make your life more manageable. There are many groups built around the twelve steps for people who grew up in dysfunctional families. The program offers a built-in structure which helps keep the meetings healthy and helpful. It's a tremendously valuable tool for change, it's available almost anywhere, and it's free except for small donations to pay for expenses such as rent.

3. Churches. The training which pastors have in counseling varies, but many of them are well-qualified to help families deal

with tough times. Some churches also sponsor support groups and classes.

4. Therapy. You'd look for treatment and help for a broken leg, asthma, or an infection. You can do the same for emotional hurts. There are counselors who specialize in family therapy, in addictions, in co-dependency, and even in helping stepfamilies. Most therapists offer individual and group sessions. Many agencies use sliding fee scales that make counseling affordable.

It's perfectly okay to check out more than one counselor until you find someone you are comfortable with. Beware of anyone who promises "quick fixes" without any effort on your part, attacks other therapeutic approaches, or implies that they have the one right answer. Ask for references and check out credentials if you have doubts. But keep in mind that most therapists are reputable and can offer you a great deal of help. If your family is struggling, therapy can be extremely valuable. Don't be afraid to give it a try.

Most of us don't think twice about going to a doctor when we hurt physically. But many people hesitate to go for help when they hurt emotionally, even though such help can be so important. Reluctance to use this kind of support is understandable. First of all, most people think they ought to be able to manage their own lives. Admitting you need help can make you feel as if you've messed up or that you are a failure. And the word "therapy" for some people still has an association with serious mental illness rather than help for ordinary people to cope with problems. The second reason is plain and simple fear. Counseling opens up your secrets and exposes your pain. It pushes you to face the issues you would prefer to ignore. It might make you change, and change is frightening.

But change is sometimes necessary. And therapy is a valuable tool that can help you make changes for the better. For a stepfamily caught in a painful pattern, professional help can make a world of difference. Asking for such help might be one of the most valuable gifts you could give yourself and other members of your blended family.

Fourteen

Is It Worth the Effort?

If your stepfamily is going to be second best anyway, is it really worth the struggle to do the best you can?

Some days, the short and only honest answer to this question is "no." Some days I'd like to talk Dean into running away to New Zealand and just forgetting the whole idea of stepfamilying. The only trouble is that, with the Internet and international telephone service, the kids could track us down anyway. "Kathleen? I forgot my backpack at Jenny's house, and we have an algebra test tomorrow." "Mom, I have to have the money for my volleyball T-shirt today." "Dad, will you take me to the Y? I know my room is a pit, but I promise I'll clean it after we get back." "But, Kathleen, it's Amy's turn to vacuum the living room this week." "How come I can't stay out all night? Everybody else gets to!"

So, what with the miracles of modern communication, we might just as well stay home. Besides, I know eventually we would both start to miss the kids.

Of course stepfamilying is sometimes a struggle. Of course it can be discouraging. But it can offer you plenty of good stuff, too. So, after a few days in beautiful New Zealand, I would have to change my answer to a definite "yes." Yes, it's worth every bit of the struggle, both for the kids and for yourself.

For the Kids

Rachel and Amy were telling me recently about a film they had seen at school on "children of divorce." The film evidently concluded that children with divorced parents had problems at school, and both girls seemed insulted by that suggestion. Rachel said indignantly, "My grades certainly didn't go down just because my parents got divorced." Then she remembered, "Of course, I guess I hadn't started school yet."

While we all laughed, I had a moment of sheer delight, mixed with relief, as I was reminded how emotionally healthy both these girls appear to be. As ninth-graders, they are into some of the emotional roller-coasters and conflict of the teenage years, and we have our tense moments. But they both do well in school, have plenty of friends, are responsible and capable, and in many other ways show every sign of turning into adults that we will be proud to launch into the world.

And that's why it's worth it. That's why it matters that parents and stepparents do the best we can.

I get annoyed when I read studies purporting to show that kids whose parents have been divorced don't do as well as kids from intact original families. These studies make me mad, because I don't think they use valid comparisons. Divorces generally happen as a result of dysfunction in the family—which means the same kids, if they had stayed in their original families, probably wouldn't be doing any better. A fairer comparison would be healthy families vs. unhealthy ones, regardless of whether the family is an original one, a single-parent one, or a stepfamily.

Even though I take such studies as a personal affront, I do know that going through the pain of divorce or the loss of a parent, followed by the chaos of a stepfamily, is terribly hard for kids. I happen to think it would be worse for many kids if they stayed in an original family which was dysfunctional. Obviously, what's better or worse is going to be different for every family and every kid. It certainly is fair to say that all kids, by the time they get to be part of a stepfamily, have gone through a substantial amount of pain.

For that reason, all of us as parents and stepparents owe it to our kids and stepkids to make our stepfamilies as healthy and strong as we can. The stakes are too high for us to do anything else.

Every adult involved with children or stepchildren has something unique to offer each child. It's your job to find whatever it is in your stepfamily that is your particular contribution. When you find that uniqueness, then use it, build on it, and be proud of it. What you do as a parent and stepparent makes an enormous difference.

A stepfamily, just because of its structure, has more than its share of chaos, conflict, and stress. That same structure, used positively, can give it some strengths. There are more adults who care about the kids. There can be shared parenting and more role models. Kids can learn flexibility, tolerance, and compassion. All of these positives only happen, of course, when the adults are mature, emotionally healthy, and committed to doing what is best for the kids. Even if the other adults involved with your stepfamily don't have that mature outlook, you can do your best to choose it for yourself. If you do, there's always a chance that others will follow your lead. Then you can all use the strengths that a healthy stepfamily offers.

I said in Chapter One that, since it takes a village to raise a child, stepfamilies are lucky because they have their own village. Make sure you do everything you can to see that your village is a strong one.

For Yourself

You can't argue with the fact that doing your best to create a healthy stepfamily is best for the kids in it. But what exactly does that do for you? Why should you work your heart out, expose

178

yourself to hurts and heartaches, and hang in there for years when you'll never be more than second best anyway? What will you get out of it, besides fatigue and some extra gray hairs?

More than you might think. There are two levels of rewards for working hard to be a good stepparent. The first one, which we've already touched on throughout this book, is developing bonds with your stepkids, adding people and love to your life, and the rich pleasure which can be part of living in a chaotic but thriving family.

The second one is less tangible but perhaps in the long run more important. It's quite simply becoming a better person. Everything you do to become a better stepparent also helps you grow emotionally and spiritually. You develop tolerance and compassion, you learn detachment and letting go, you work toward accepting life's difficulty with grace and humor. And along the way, you just keep getting better and better.

One of my favorite posters says, "It's easy to be an angel as long as nobody ruffles your feathers." When life is uncomplicated, it's easy to think of yourself as a good person who is always kind and patient and just plain wonderful. But you don't really develop any of those qualities if you don't have any challenges. Of course you can be serene if you live with nobody but a cat and you don't let yourself be exposed to any of life's rough roads. But I don't happen to believe that's what we're here for.

When you get to the end of your life, and you look back on who you have been and what you have done, what exactly do you want to see? What impact do you want to have during your life? The kind of stepparent you choose to be is an important part of the answers to those questions. You can look at being part of a stepfamily as a burden, a nuisance, or an impediment to your own plans. Or you can look at it as an opportunity to grow and as an important part of your own journey toward maturity.

So go ahead and do the best you can. Use all of your courage, your energy, and your capacity to love. The rewards may not come back to you immediately or in the form you might expect. But they will come. The pain, the struggles, and the heartaches which can come with stepfamilying are worth it when you use them to become the kind of person you are capable of being.

Enjoy and appreciate your second-place medal. You will have earned it. And, when you do everything you can to build a strong and healthy stepfamily, you'll know in your heart that there is nothing second-best about you.

ADDITIONAL RESOURCES

Stepfamily Association of America
650 J. Street, Suite 205
Lincoln, NE 68508
800-735-0329
　　　This organization publishes a quarterly newsletter, has a catalog of books and tapes for purchase, and offers help in starting local stepfamily support groups.

BOOKS:

Strengthening Your Stepfamily
Elizabeth Einstein and Linda Albert
American Guidance Service, Circle Pines, MN 55014

Stepfamily Realities: How to Overcome Difficulties and Have a Happy Family
Margaret Newman
New Harbinger, 1994

Making Peace in Your Stepfamily
Harold H. Bloomfield, M.D.
Hyperion, 1993

Remarriage and Your Money
Patricia Schiff Estess
Little, Brown and Company, 1992

Perfect Parenting and Other Myths
Frank Main, Ed.D.
Prairie Flower Press, 509 Valley View, Vermillion, SD 57069
605-677-5257

Love and Power in the Stepfamily
Jamie Keshet
McGraw Hill, 1987
(This book unfortunately is out of print; check your local library.)

The Road Less Traveled
M. Scott Peck, M.D.
Simon and Schuster, 1978

ORDER FORM

For additional copies of *Making the Best of Second Best,* send this form and a check or money order for $13.95 ($11.95 plus $2.00 shipping and handling) to:

FoxCraft, Inc.
PO Box 7822
Rapid City, SD 57709

(Please print)

Name _____

Address _____

City, State, Zip _____

Number of copies: _____   Amount enclosed: _____

You can place a credit card order through our website at www.foxcraftinc.com. Check out the website, too, for information on additional self-help and parenting books.